Suwarow's Campaign of 1799

COUNT ALEXANDER VASILYEVICH SUWAROW

Suwarow's Campaign of 1799

Russia's Victory Over France in Italy & Switzerland
During the War of the Second Coalition

ILLUSTRATED

Edward Nevil Macready

LEONAUR

Suwarow's Campaign of 1799
Russia's Victory Over France in Italy & Switzerland During the War of the Second Coalition
by Edward Nevil Macready

ILLUSTRATED

First published under the title
Sketch of Suwarow, and His Last Campaign

Leonaur is an imprint of Oakpast Ltd

Copyright in this form © 2021 Oakpast Ltd

ISBN: 978-1-78282-996-6 (hardcover)
ISBN: 978-1-78282-997-3 (softcover)

http://www.leonaur.com

Publisher's Notes

Contents

Contents

Prefatory Notice by the Editor

It was the purpose of the late Major Macready to illustrate the account of Suwarow's last and brilliant campaign by plans of his actions and important operations, corrected from personal examination of the localities: and we have to regret that he did not live either to fulfil this intention, or to give a final revision to his MS. The memoir is now printed from a transcript by Mrs. Edward Macready, which she placed in the editor's hands, accompanied by her husband's private journals; a perusal of which has led him to form a very high estimate of the writer, both as a soldier and a man. The following were the leading incidents in the career of this accomplished officer.

In 1814, at the age of sixteen, he joined, as a volunteer, the second battalion 30th Regiment, then serving in Holland under Lord Lynedoch, and in the following year he fought both at Quatre Bras and Waterloo; commanding the Light Company towards the close of the great battle, when only an ensign. The gallantry he displayed on these memorable occasions procured his promotion to a lieutenancy.

His next active service was in India, where he took part in the assault and capture of the strong fortress of Asseerghur, although labouring at the time under so severe an illness, that it was with the utmost difficulty he could obtain permission to share in the attack. His journal of this period is very interesting, both as giving a most graphic description of the country traversed, and also containing opinions of men and measures, by a mind of no ordinary stamp.

On the appointment of Sir John Wilson to the Staff of Ceylon, the Commander-in-Chief, Lord Hill, recommended Captain Macready as Military Secretary, solely from the favourable opinion he had formed of his zeal, abilities, and professional acquirements.

The following extract from a speech of the governor of the island, the Right Hon. Stewart McKenzie, will serve to show how ably Captain Macready filled that office:—

> Nor can I pass over in silence the services of the Military Sec-
> retary, of which, at the same time that we shall lose the able
> assistance and advice of our gallant Commander of the Forces
> and trusty Counsellor, Sir John Wilson, we are soon to be de-
> prived: for an abler and more excellent officer in the depart-
> ment he occupies, than Captain Macready, is rarely to be met
> with; combining, with assiduity in business and accuracy in its
> details, a fairness which always renders access to him at all times,
> and discussion with him of all matters, easy and profitable. With
> Captain Macready, our Colonial Secretary has for a long pe-
> riod held constant and varied communications on official busi-
> ness, without one interruption by serious difference. I the more
> readily embrace this occasion to offer this tribute, due to the
> character and services of Captain Macready, in his presence and
> in yours, who form so large a body of the civilians of Ceylon,
> because I am confident that you, and my honourable guest, will
> be equally eager to confirm what I am about to add:—that it
> will be no easy task to fill his situation with his equal—with
> any one surpassing him in the essential qualities of an intelli-
> gent officer and a gentleman, which distinguish Captain Mac-
> ready, I am persuaded it cannot be filled.

In addition to this public testimony of his services and character
from the lips of the governor, he received a private tribute to his
worth, in the form of a handsome piece of plate, in the names of *"his
friends;"* which title comprehended, we believe, every officer then at
Ceylon. This was the most gratifying event of his life.

On further promotion, he quitted the 30th, in which he was en-
deared to all, and withdrew from military service: Colonel Slade, long
afterwards, writes:

> But not forgotten, for often and often when I have praised the
> appearance of the Light Company, the answer has been, 'Oh!
> Macready infused a spirit into that company, which they have
> retained ever since.'

Leisure being now afforded him to indulge the long-cherished
desire of visiting scenes of important military operations, he went
abroad, and trod many a battlefield in Germany, Italy, and Switzerland.
Being dissatisfied with the versions of Suwarow's last Campaign by

French, Austrian, and even English writers, he resolved that tardy justice should be done to the Russian hero; and accordingly penned the following able disquisition.

It must be distinctly understood that the editor has simply sought to fulfil the intentions of the author; scrupulously abstaining from doing more than striving to render the sense clear. All essentials remain untouched: had he felt warranted to alter anything, he might have ventured to soften some of the expressions used in reference to a distinguished British historian.

NORTH ITALY
AND
SWITZERLAND
1796--1805
English Miles
0 10 20 30 40 50

Introduction

As at this moment (1847) considerations of a military nature are occupying attention in England, the following sketch, compiled by an idle soldier for his own satisfaction, during a course of professional reading, is submitted to the public.

Suwarow especially admired the English, because he believed them to be brave, earnest, and honest; and for the same qualities does the Writer admire the character of Suwarow, feeling confidently persuaded, that the more his spirit infuses itself into the mind and heart of any man, the better man and soldier will he prove. There are few that will not smile at the eccentricities, or listen with compassionate interest to the misfortunes, of this strangely constituted man; but to the soldier more particularly, or to him who looks to be one, the mixed nature of his military qualities, presents a pleasing and repaying subject of contemplation.

Suwarow cannot rank with those who have thrown new light upon tactics or strategy; nor does he astonish and delight us by those simple and sublime combinations of battle, which multiply the chances and the consequences of victory. The words "forward and strike," in his estimation, condensed the better half of what could be learnt of war: "system-mongers," "precise talkers,"—"*scribentismus*," and "*methodismus*,"—were the terms in which, from his own peculiar vocabulary, he expressed his contempt for the military theory of his day, and its admirers.

His professional career had commenced in the Seven Years' War, in which he witnessed glorious opportunities lost, and gross absurdities defended, by an adherence to the rules of an erroneous system. It was at Kunersdorf, that he first saw fire, and there the desperate courage of his countrymen, in their broken masses, baffled one of the ablest dispositions of the immortal Frederick.

This early experience, therefore, as well as his after service against the Turks and Poles, equally tended to strengthen the bias of his mind, which led him to calculate on rapidity and valour alone, and to undervalue the mighty influence of scientific combinations. He grew up a zealot in his honest bigotry to this prejudice; which, like every other prejudice, repaid his devotion with injury: it stamped him a general of the secondary class.

But his mind and actions are not the less deserving our consideration. He is a glorious instance of what may be effected by the energetic development and exercise of qualities, the germs of which are in almost every human heart. Examples of a loftier class may readily be found, but none of more general application. His faults (at once so serious and so palpable) convey a universal lesson. His excellences every soldier may aspire to emulate. The first show us how incumbent on us is the study of our art; the second, what earnest courage and devotion can effect towards covering with success our greatest errors. These qualities dignify our nature, by elevating a common energy to a level (as far as regards results) with rare and accidental gifts of intellect; they teach confidence to the soldier who distrusts his ability, by showing irrefutably that to strike strongly is next to striking skilfully; and they bid him "on and fear not;" secure in the conviction that if his country be not benefited by his talent it will at least by the example of his devotion.

The sketch of the character of Suwarow has been attempted, in the hope of adding to the interest of the military details that follow it; our assent to abstract truth being frequently the extent of its effect upon us, whereas an illustration that awakens our sympathy may produce a deeper, and occasionally an influential, impression.

The authorities consulted have been chiefly Duboscage, Dumas, Segur, Jomini, St. Cyr, the Archduke Charles, and Suwarow's published correspondence; and the writer has visited most of the ground of which he has occasion to speak.

CHAPTER 1

A Sketch of Suwarow

Suwarow, in the sixty-ninth year of his age and the second of his banishment from the court of St. Petersburg, was leading an almost patriarchal life on his estate of Khantschansk, attending to agricultural matters, arranging the disputes, and not unfrequently the marriages and love affairs of his peasants, and accomplishing himself in the arts of psalm-singing and church-bell ringing, by a diligent and public practice of both, when, in February 1799, an official despatch addressed to "Field-Marshal Suwarow" was put into his hands. He said:

This is not for me, a field-marshal is at the head of armies. I am nothing but an old soldier called Suwarow.

And he returned the letter. Some days later, a similar packet, addressed "to my faithful subject Suwarow," was presented to him, and he read:—

I have resolved to send you into Italy to the assistance of His Majesty the Emperor and King, my brother and ally. Suwarow has no need of triumphs nor of laurels, but the country has need of him, and my wishes agree with those of Francis II., who having conferred on you the supreme command of his Italian Army, begs you to accept that dignity. It depends on Suwarow alone to satisfy the hopes of his country and the desire of the Emperor Paul I.

But little enthusiasm is requisite to imagine the old man's transport, as with a bounding heart he hurried over the words of this unexpected and welcome commission; nor can even the chivalrous Francis, as he leapt into the saddle and scoured along the plain, joyously proclaiming himself "once more a king," be deemed more enviable in the wild rapture of his exultation, than poor Suwarow at that recompensing moment. It gave him freedom, and it promised glory; and in the fervour of his emotion, he pressed the letter to his heart and to his wounds, and crying aloud, "It is new life to me," accepted the appointment.

Suwarow's devotion and loyalty were those of a Russian soldier of his day. He looked on the revolutionary French as the apostles of anarchy and irreligion, for his sovereign ("the God on earth" of every true Muscovite) had declared them to be so, and he had a standard in his own energy by which he could appreciate their baneful power. He said to a French nobleman:

> Do you know why the Jacobins triumph? It is because their will is strong and deep—to succeed, it must be undivided. You *émigres* don't half will.

The constant wish of his heart was to meet these enemies of God and man in battle. He often wrote to Catherine:

> Lady mother, let me march against the French.

★★★★★★

Note:—The Empress Catherine had banished every Frenchman from her dominions who would not swear eternal hatred to the Republic. She had courted the Academicians as long as they amused her with mere speculative discussions, or pleased her by contrasting the good she had done for her subjects, with the abuses to which the great in other lands clung with irrational and perilous pertinacity. There was, in fact, a generalisation in the doctrines, as in the terms of "Philosophy, Reason, and Liberty," which allured very many of the privileged classes to aid in their development, almost as ardently as the patriot or the demagogue. But there was no mistaking the word "Equality"—the most tremendous in import and effect that the voice of man has uttered. It was the war-cry of every political hope and interest in Europe. "*Je suis aristocrate: il faute fair mon métier,*" was the declaration of the imperturbable Catherine.

★★★★★★

When, in 1796, Buonaparte's successes were the daily subjects of conversation, he constantly repeated:

> Yes, that youngster goes too fast, it is full time to stop him.

In 1798, he was confidently persuaded that the policy of the

18

French Directory, both at home and abroad, had rendered the capture of Paris and the restoration of the Bourbons easily attainable by the powers coalesced against France, provided only they would set themselves heart and soul to the work; and on the 17th Sept. he dictated the following memorandum on the subject, to his friend M. General Prevot de Lumian:

Austria and Russia should act against France with 100,000 men, on the following principles:—1st. Nothing to be thought of but the offensive—2nd. Quick marches; energy in attack; the naked steel—3rd. No theory (methodik); *Coup d'oeil*—4th. Full powers to the general-in-chief—5th. Seek the enemy in the field and beat him—6th. Lose no time in sieges, unless in coming on a grand depot (as Mayence); if necessary, now and then blockade a place, and occasionally carry a fortress by surprise or storm. Time and men are saved by this—7th. Never scatter forces to cover many points. If the enemy passes the unguarded points, so much the better; he comes to us to be crushed—8th. An observation corps is only necessary at Strasburg, and a flying corps near Luxembourg.

When one has to go forward, there should be no halting. Push direct on Paris as the grand point—do not halt before Landau, but observe it with a sufficient force—not to cover a retreat, which must not be thought of, but to protect the convoys. There must be no idle manoeuvring, countermarches, and what are called *ruses de guerre*. Such things are only fit for wretched pedants—9th. Italy and the Netherlands fall easily after Paris. The King of Sardinia declares himself against France. There are still madmen enough in Italy, but all but they are for the good cause. The King of Naples will be alive again. The English clear the Mediterranean. No delay! False prudence and envy are the Medusa heads of cabinets and ministries.

After a solemn thanksgiving for his good fortune, the field-marshal hastened to St. Petersburg to pay his duty to his sovereign. The interview was short and embarrassing—painful to Suwarow and humiliating to Paul. The faithful veteran, recalled by the necessities of his country from an exile, the reward of his valour and devotion, knelt before his master, at once the memorial of his ingratitude and the dependence of his hope. Neither party was anxious to prolong the conference. Suwarow with all his loyalty, could not respect the emperor; and Paul was too conscious of his own injustice, ever sincerely to forgive the object of it. The circumstances of their misunderstanding were these:—during Paul's reformation of the Russian costume, Suwarow received a package of sticks as models of the tails and curls, which, with the addition of powder, were to adorn the troops under his command. The conqueror of the Turks and Poles replied to this extraordinary despatch with three lines, which may be freely rendered:—

The tails have not the bayonet's powers,
The curls are not long twenty-fours,
The barber's powder is not ours.

Bad as these are (and the originals are little better), it was a severe canon of criticism that punished them with banishment. But it was the ill fortune of the Emperor Paul to miscalculate on hiding the fears that haunted him, by a wilful and eccentric exercise of his authority; and unhappily these timid experiments, in almost every instance, fell more heavily on his true and faithful subjects than on his enemies.

On receiving his sentence of banishment, the obedient warrior assembled his troops, and took leave of them; concluding thus:—

I do not despair but that the emperor, our common father, will one day relent, in consideration of my age. Then, when Suwarow shall reappear among you, he will resume these badges, (taking off all his brilliant orders) which he leaves you as a pledge of his friendship, and as a token of your remembrance. You will not forget that he wore them in the victories to which he led you.

At these words he laid them on the drums in front of the line, and retired amidst the tears and groans of the soldiery. It was a day of delight, such as none but a chief like him, or a soldier who has followed one whose word was victory, can well imagine, when he rode once more among them as their leader.

But little time was lost in gratulation; he hurried onward towards Vienna, and at Mittau paid his respects to Louis XVIII., declaring "that would be the happiest day of his life, in which he should pour forth the last drop of his blood, to place him on the throne of his ancestors." The Emperor Francis received him with distinguished honours, and the Austrian troops who had christened him on the bloodstained field of Fokschau, welcomed with acclamations their old deliverer, "General Vorwärts." The emperor asked what was his plan of operations, he replied: "I never make any, Your Majesty, time, place, and circumstances decide me."

"You must have some plan," continued Francis; "I wish to know it."

Suwarow smiled and said, "If I had, sire, I should not tell it; Your Majesty's council would know it this evening, and the enemy tomorrow." So steadily did Suwarow adhere to his views on this point, that the emperor, to the great dissatisfaction of his minister, Baron Thugut, was forced to assent to his demand that he should act in all respects independently of the council of war, and only communicate his views direct to the emperor himself.

Speaking on this subject to Duboscage, Suwarow said,—

When the Empress Catherine honoured me with the command of armies, she did so because she thought I could lead them to victory. How could she judge better than an old soldier on the spot, how that victory could be won? When I received orders that were contrary to her interests, I considered them as suggested by courtiers or enemies, and I acted according to what I thought conducive to her glory.

★★★★★★

Note:—Duboscage adds an anecdote of a very gallant, but glaring disobedience on the part of Suwarow, who reported it, forwarding his sword and writing:—"As a soldier, I am guilty; as a Russian, I have done my duty, &c" The less said on such matters the better. The rule is wise and positive against them; but the exceptions are so brilliant, so heart-stirring; there is such an entire devotedness in them, that, perhaps, many will say, with a young friend of mine:—"I would sentence the man who did so to be shot; but I would do it, and be proud to be shot for it myself."

★★★★★★

The man who acted thus towards sovereigns, was in person miserably thin, and five feet one inch in height. A large mouth, pug nose, eyes commonly half shut, a few grey side locks, brought over the top of his bald crown, and a small unpowdered queue, the whole surmounted by a three-cornered felt hat ornamented with green fringe, composed the "head and front" of Field-Marshal Suwarow; but his eyes when open, were piercing, and in battle they were said to be terrifically expressive.

When anything said or done, displeased him, a wavy play of his deeply wrinkled forehead betrayed, or rather expressed, his disapproval. He had a philosophical contempt of dress, and might often be seen drilling his men in his shirt sleeves. It was only during the severest weather that he wore cloth, his outer garments being usually of white serge turned up with green. These were most indifferently made, as were his large, coarsely greased slouching boots; one of which he very commonly dispensed with, leaving his knee-band unbuttoned, and his stocking about his heel. A huge sabre and a single order completed his ordinary costume; but on grand occasions his field-marshal's uniform was covered with badges, and he was fond of telling where and how he had won them.

He often arose at midnight, and welcomed the first soldier he saw moving, with a piercing imitation of the crowing of a cock, in compliment to his early rising. It is said that, in the first Polish war, knowing a spy was in camp, he issued orders for an attack at cock-crow, and the enemy expecting it in the morning, were cut to pieces at nine at night; Suwarow having turned out the troops an hour before, by his well-known cry. The evening before the storm of Ismail he informed his columns:

Tomorrow morning, an hour before daybreak, I mean to get up,
I shall then dress and wash myself, then say my prayers, and then
give one good cock-crow and capture Ismail!

When Segur asked him if he never took off his clothes at night, he replied, "No! when I get lazy and want to have a comfortable sleep, I generally take off one spur." Buckets of cold water were thrown over him before he dressed, and his table was served at seven or eight o'clock with sandwiches and various messes which Duboscage describes as "*des ragouts Kosaks détestables;*" to which men paid "the mouth honour, which they would fain deny, but dare not," lest Suwarow should consider them effeminate.

He had been very sickly in his youth, but by spare diet and cold bathing had strengthened and hardened himself into first-rate condition. English ale was his favourite drink. Soldiers, indifferently from any regiment, were his servants. His food, straw (for he used no bed), and lodging were the same as theirs. He saluted as they did, dispensed with pocket-handkerchiefs, like them; would be seen half-naked, airing his shirt and dressing himself at a watch fire, among a crowd of them: in short, he adopted all their habits. Descending to be their friend and model, he did not only what they were obliged to do, but whatever it was to their advantage should be done; and they were proud to imitate the man who was not less their comrade than their commander, and the companion of princes. The constraint of duty was unfelt—obedience was a delight to them. They called themselves his children, and him their father, and while he attended to their wants like one, his familiar jests with them, or in their presence, made every condescension convey some lesson. He observed:

What I say to a soldier is told to his comrades at night, and next day the army know it.

To impress on them the duty of implicit obedience, his *aides-de-camp* were accustomed to interrupt his dinner or his doze with "you must eat no more," or "you must walk."

"Ah!" he would answer in affected surprise, "by whose order?"

"By that of Field-Marshal Suwarow," was the reply; and "he must be obeyed," was the laughing and submissive rejoinder.

He once had his arm raised to strike a soldier, when an officer boldly exclaimed, "The field-marshal has commanded that no one shall give way to passion," he desisted, saying "What the field-marshal orders, Suwarow obeys."

His instructions tended to form the man as well as the soldier:

If you perceive a cannon with lighted match, rush upon it creeping, the ball will pass over your head—cannon and cannoniers are your own—overset the gun and spike it—the men may receive quarter. It is a sin to slay without a cause. Do no wrong to an unoffending: party. He supplies you with meat and drink. A true soldier is no robber. Spoil is to be held sacred—if you capture a camp or fortress, it is all your own; but beware of laying your hands upon spoil without previous orders. Seek to die for the honour of the Virgin Mary—your mother (the empress), and all the royal family. The church offers up prayers for those who fall—honours and rewards await those who live. A soldier should be healthy-minded, brave, intrepid, decisive, loyal and honourable. Let him pray to God, from whom proceed victory and miraculous interpositions. God be our guide! God is our leader!

"I don't know—I can't—impossible—" were words he hated: "learn—

do—try—" he would exclaim. When a soldier is expected to act, and does nothing, he must do wrong—if he does something, there are chances he does rightly. Many a man has resources within himself that he is not aware of. Under Suwarow he was sure to do his best.

If he went into a house, when the army bivouacked, he frequently ordered away the doors and windows. "I am not cold nor afraid," he would say, and the soldiers who laughed as they obeyed the order, would try to brave the cold like "their father." When provisions were very scarce, he not unfrequently met the difficulty by ordering a general fast; which, as he kept it religiously, was cheerfully acquiesced in by the men.

The extremes of courage and endurance were spoken of by him, before them, as common-place exertions. Soldiers marched and fought till they fell, as a matter of course. He has said:

> I often march forty miles, the general is with the head—the head never waits for the tail—I leave stragglers behind—the worse for them—they miss the victory. The brave fellows who keep up, are always enough to surprise and beat the enemy.

In thirty-six hours, he marched twenty-four leagues with cannon, to Fokschany, and arriving there at five o'clock; his order of battle, issued at eleven, began: "troops having rested, will march at two, to attack the enemy."

In Poland, in 1769, his force marched nearly 300 miles in twelve days, and as much in 1771, fighting almost every second day. His ordinary routine of march in Italy, was for the cooks and provisions to move on at midnight, two German miles. At three in the morning the troops marched a mile, then rested an hour, and marched the other mile to their cooks; where, in Suwarow's words, "Food is ready—wine is there—not a marauder to be heard of." After four hours' rest, another mile was marched—then another halt, and another mile marched brought the troops to their ground—and at three next morning they were again *en route*. In directing Bellegarde to adopt this practice, Suwarow's concluding words are:

> Hasten, Your Excellency—money is valuable—man's life much more so—but the most valuable of all is time.

When the fire of battle opened on the Russians, the solemn murmur of "God have mercy upon us," rose along the line; and Suwarow, stationed on some conspicuous spot, always crossed himself and reverentially kissed the picture of St. Nicholas, to add the stimulus of his soldiers' love to him (for all believed he would not survive defeat) to that admirable sense of duty, which saw no alternative in battle, but the triumph of their earthly, or the judgment of their heavenly master. He has cried aloud, when a fight went badly:

> I must die!—I cannot live if it be lost.

At Kinburn, in 1787, when desperately wounded, seeing his troops in confusion, he left his litter and mounted to rally them; and when his efforts to restore order seemed ineffectual, he threw himself from his horse, almost among the Turks, calling to his own men:

> Run, do run! and leave your wounded general to the enemy.

Even in the conflict's fiercest fury, nothing that affected his children's progress could escape him. He once exclaimed as they seemed to shrink before some Turks:

> Never look at their eyes, boys, look at their breasts, there's the mark for your bayonets.

He practised no retreat movements, and hardly any firings. Charles XII. used to say, "don't fire, friends: let cowards do that," Suwarow's expression was "the ball's a fool, the bayonet a hero."

He drilled his people to charge, infantry against infantry or cavalry indifferently, and cavalry against horse or foot. In the midst of a tremendous fire of artillery, with loud shouts of "Forward, forward! hurrah, hurrah! the sabre! the bayonet! never fear, boys! forward, forward!" would they press onward against each other, as if in battle, the infantry at *the pas de charge*, the cavalry at the trot and gallop. At the moment of meeting, the bayonets were thrown up, and the foot soldiers making a half-turn, passed each other. The cavalry files were loosened for this purpose, and the horses in all cases were made to break through the body against which they charged; but knees were crushed, horsemen dismounted, and sometimes sabre cuts exchanged in this rough training, which Suwarow never saw. (Marshal Marmont, in his work, *De l'Esprit des Institutions Militaires*, strongly recommends a course of drill precisely similar to this of Suwarow's, but without acknowledging it to have been Suwarow's practice.)

The artillery exerted themselves so earnestly to keep up with the infantry, that Duboscage saw five men accidentally killed or maimed on one occasion at a single gun, without any delay occurring in its advance.

Forts were constructed, palisaded, and covered with *abattis, trous de loup*, &c., and in the attack and defence of these, the troops were practised both by day and night. Figures of straw and clay were put up in every quarter, and Suwarow's smile rewarded him whose sabre cut the deepest. In the bayonet practice, his personal feelings were oddly shown. At the words "charge on the Poles," the recruit advanced and gave a thrust; at "charge on the Prussians," the recruit stabbed twice (Suwarow hated the military foppery and pretension of that people); at "charge on the French," ("the light, skipping, God-forgetting French" he called them) the recruit stabbed twice horizontally, and once downwards into the ground. When the victim was supposed to be a Turk, the soldier was cautioned in addition, to shake him from the bayonet: "he must be very dead," Suwarow used to say, "when he does not try a sweeping cut."

All his drill was applicable to actual battle, where the men had to conquer or die. It was their interest to kill fast, and they were taught what was at once best for themselves and "for the honour and safety of their sovereign and his dominions."

★★★★★★

Note:—The following anecdote, from Duboscage, reminds one of the lancers in the rear of Henry of Trastamare's army, who, according to Froissart, "Kept up the courage of the combatants, by driving such as fled back to their divisions." A colonel of cavalry having dropped behind his people in a charge, Suwarow called to the Cossacks near him:—"Look! a colonel behind his men! He'll be taken by the *infidels*—what a disgrace to us. Kill him!—kill him!—kill him!" The Cossacks were off, pike in hand; but before their speed could bring them to the colonel, he had driven both spurs into his horse, and was in front of his men, leading them like a hero into a cloud of Turks.

★★★★★★

The absolutely defensive in war, is an absurdity. A weak force spread out to cover many points, exposes itself to be inevitably pierced and beaten. Mass it, and occupy the most important points, and act vigorously, as opportunities offer; this is still more advisable if your force be strong. An army disseminated like men on a chessboard, each portion to support another, may be ruined by the cowardice, stupidity or caprice of any one of its constituent parts. Force is multiplied by activity—a rapid march will seldom find an enemy prepared for battle; if it does, a general with *coup d'oeil* and good troops, can make his dispositions. The fire of infantry is for defence—the bayonet for attack. All killed by an exchange of fire, after lines or columns of attack can be formed, are uselessly sacrificed. While bodies fire, the loss is tolerably equal; it is in the pursuit that casualties preponderate. Bad troops stand fire; few good ones stand the bayonet; those that do, can hardly use it too soon. The leader of an army is its genius! He must not be made the tool of pen-and-ink men (*scribentismus*). Their plans of campaign may be eloquent, but they are not natural: they may be fine, but they are not good: they may look brilliant, but they are not to be reckoned on. It is the commander-in-chief who alone can appreciate and decide on the unforeseen contingencies of war, as they occur. He must not hesitate—must be indefatigable: he alone must direct his troops. Nobody—nothing should shackle him. He must be without self-love. On him the fate of all must rest.

Those were the opinions with which Suwarow sought his enemy, and he could depend upon his soldiers and upon himself.

Science is nothing but a record of the best deductions from human sagacity and experiment, and as human reason is not infallible, there may be *soi-disant* systems that are based on error. Such Suwarow deemed the system he ridiculed; but we are not for that reason to suppose that in his proceedings he never adopted plans, from his own sagacity and reflection, which the rules of science would approve.

All his battles in Italy were fought on the one simple and uniform principle of an advance in direct *échelon* from his right; and alike at the Adda, the Trebbia, and at Noir, this was the proceeding which true science would have dictated. He scoffed at "system-mongers, precise-talkers, Demosthenes, Hannibal's senate, *scribentismus*, and the hellish abysses of *methodismus*," because he very commonly found those who preached theory, to him or to the world, slow to do and backward to dare, and because they quoted "words of exceeding good command" from their theoretical vocabularies, in justification of their short-comings. On such science he pronounced, like Corporal Trim on Captain Tripet's peculiar evolutions, that "one home thrust of the bayonet was worth the whole of it."

A system like Suwarow's has an essential tendency to degenerate into rashness; for extraordinary successes induce extravagant expectations, and where so much is referred to courage (the effects of which depend less on its own intrinsic power than on the weaknesses of others) calculation must occasionally be disappointed. But seldom, even in his last campaign (when he came, weakened by age, to the encounter of his most formidable antagonist) do we find his dispositions exacting more than his troops could well perform.

It was not rashness to hurry an attack at Rymnik, when every hour strengthened his enemy's entrenchments; nor to surprise by an assault, the confident valour that declared "the Danube should stay its course, and the heavens bow to earth, before Ismail surrendered." Months had already been lost before that fortress, when Potemkin ordered Suwarow to carry it in a given number of days. "The will of the empress must be obeyed," said he; and at the appointed time he wrote:

The Russian flag waves over Ismail.

This capture, and those of Bender and Oczakoff illustrate most remarkably the want of science and the excess of courage in Catherine's armies. All these towns were besieged for months—in none was a breach effected; at each, the troops (in one case almost mutinously) called for the assault, and all were carried; neither of the storms costing 5,000 men, whereas eight times that number had been expended in the procedures called sieges. A breach is likely to be as hard to win from Turks as a wall, and it is certain to be far more closely watched. The siege of Acre is a study for those who cavil at the storm of Ismail.

Suwarow's daring exploits, both against Turks and Poles, were based on a thorough knowledge of his own troops, and of the military deficiencies of those people. The artillery of both was contemptible: the one religiously adhered to the barbarous tactics of their ancestors, while the other was a mob of noblemen too proud to be obedient soldiers, or of slaves too degraded at once to become brave ones. Rhulière, the historian of the fall of Poland, says somewhat naively of these latter:

Ils ne connaissent point cette insensibilité stupide avec laquelle les Russes se laissent ôter leur misérable vie, dont ils ne croient pas avoir la propriété.
Les Russes n'hésitaient jamais, quelque fut leur petit nombre, à marcher au premier avis centre tout parti Polonais.

It requires an effort of the imagination to conceive what could be rashness, under such circumstances.

Suwarow, trusting to his Cossacks to guarantee him from surprise, seldom reconnoitred, or patrolled to any great distance. Parties for either purpose, he was accustomed to say, tell more by their appearance than they learn by their observation. He had a still stronger objection to *parleys*, or communications under flags of truce. He would say contemptuously:

Parlementaires! An Austrian receives one, and while he *parleys*, the French cross the Rhine and beat his division; he has scarcely done his *parley*, when he finds himself a prisoner.

A *parley* is usually an admission of weakness, or an attempt to overreach. In the one case, the enemy hopes to give less than he knows his antagonist can take; on the other, to keep him in inaction. In both, it is safer to act, than to treat.

Ridiculously enough, the slaughter attendant on his successes, has been made the subject of Suwarow's vituperation; as if any but the weak or treacherous would hesitate to take the most effectual means against the enemies of his country. Suwarow conquered Poland in two months; it had been well for that unhappy land if Repnin and Weymann had done so. (See note following.)

★★★★★★

Note:—Prince Repnin was ambassador at Warsaw during the previous protracted war, and Poland was fallen indeed, when he survived the outrages and insults, he had heaped upon her. But none are all evil. His brother, the general, being taken by the Turks, was not employed again, and died broken-hearted. The prince followed him to the grave, and looking for the last time on his remains, he said, "No; you shall not become dust without some mark of honour"—casting on the coffin a splendid honorary sword, the reward of one of his own triumphs, he continued, "You were at least as worthy of it as I." This is touching, but it would not be believed in Poland.

★★★★★★

Suwarow observed:

I have three ways of treating an enemy, when he meets me and we are reconciled, he is my friend, my brother; when he opposes me, and capitulates he is my prisoner; when we cross swords, he dies. Thus, the terror of my arms diminishes the number of my enemies, and one bloody battle prevents many others that might be more so.

It was acknowledged by his enemies that he was kind to prisoners; that he welcomed them to his table, and severely punished such of his own army as ill-treated them; but writers on Poland have vilified him, because he was in that country (what every soldier is liable to be) the champion of an atrocious policy. We find him nicknamed Muley Is-mael, after a Moorish emperor of that name who was a great shedder of blood, because much was shed before the capture of Ismail was effected.

During the operations of that siege, Suwarow was so unlucky as to say to his men, "Provisions are scarce, boys; yonder merry fellows are choking with them; come now, let us take the town": and this jocular expression has not only been condensed, in Castera's history of Cath-erine, into "no quarter, provisions are dear"; but the author proceeds to charge Suwarow with "putting to the sword all the inhabitants of Praga, without distinction of age or sex," adding that "the barbarian entered Warsaw covered with the blood of these unfortunates." The solitary truth in this comprehensive passage, seems to be the fact that Suwarow entered Warsaw; which, however, he did not for a week after the assault of Praga. The fifteenth article of the orders for that attack, runs thus:—

We must act with the greatest energy against such as bear arms: but the inhabitants, the men without arms, and such as ask for quarter, will be spared.

Sad atrocities are committed at every storm—humanity and dis-cipline are alike forgotten on such occasions by the soldiery of every nation; but when the deputation from Warsaw stood before Suwarow, after the fall of Praga, confused and silent (for they had to account to the Russians for the massacre of their comrades), he threw down his sabre, and stepping on it, clasped the nearest of them in his arms, saying in Polish:—

Peace, peace: I am not come to destroy you—name your terms, I will accept them.

An officer of his staff insists that he had the bridge between Praga and Warsaw in part shot away, to prevent the sack of the capital; but, however we may discredit this, it is certain that he allowed the Poles to continue negotiations longer than was deemed advisable by his brother officers, who recommended him to seize Potocki as an hos-tage. He exclaimed:

What's a hostage good for? Besides, it would be criminal—he came here on the faith of the armistice.

When at length conditions were agreed upon, and he entered Warsaw in triumph, on the keys being presented to him he was heard to say:—

Almighty God, I thank thee that I have not bought these keys as dearly as——

He turned towards Praga—his eyes filled with tears, and the words died away upon his lips. And this was not cant: who was there for Suwarow to cant before? He feared no man, he braved the prejudices of the great, and when he practised insinuation, it was to make the lowly happy. He was uncompromising and straight-forward: when he differed with men, he told them so; when he despised them, he showed he did so. Being called to court by Catherine, people of whom he knew nothing crowded round him, full of professions of sympathy and friendship; he disentangled himself from them to walk up to a dirty stove-heater, and embraced him, requesting his esteem and countenance, he remarked:—

I am on new ground here, and they tell me everyone at court may be dangerous.

The Emperor Paul one day sent to him Count de Kutaijoff, a menial Turk whom he had ennobled; and Suwarow, turning to his attendant, thus addressed him:—

Iwan, you see this nobleman—he has been what you are, he is now a count, and wears orders. It is true he has been near the person of our gracious sovereign: but behave well, Iwan; who knows what you may come to be?

Suwarow has been called avaricious, whereas he set so little value on money that he scarcely meddled with it. Colonel Sichinka, who had saved his life when a private, managed his household affairs; and not only provided him with the detestable ragouts before mentioned, but (much to his own advantage, it is said) with "shirts to his body, horse to ride, and weapon to wear." His extraordinary disinterestedness might have been no virtue, for it was no effort. He accepted no lands from Catherine until after he had children; and when she was distributing favours at Kresnentschouk, and asked him, "Do you want nothing, general?"

31

CATHERINE II, (CATHERINE THE GREAT)

"Nothing, Your Majesty," he replied, "unless you'll order me my lodging-money," a few *roubles*.

An officer of his staff at Warsaw, in 1794, having misapplied a very considerable sum of money, Suwarow punished him and paid the amount. "It is just," he observed, "that I answer for those I employ."

In 1796, he made an application to Catherine, through his son-in-law Zouboff, in favour of a deserving officer. Zouboff neglected the business, and Suwarow wrote to him:—

I see my request was ill-timed. I have given an estate to the officer. I shall always do thus. Rich as we are by the bounty of the empress, it is but right that we should share our fortune with those who serve her well.

On being banished, he offered to surrender a large estate to Paul; and on his recall, he sent for a rich peasant with whom he often conversed, and said to him:—

See the goodness of God—a little hour ago I was in disgrace, now I am a chief of armies. I know your friendship, and I wish you to share my happiness. Lend me 100 *roubles* for this campaign—there's no knowing what may happen, and its prudent to have money by one.

Though his language was often harsh, we sometimes find a dignified courteousness in his style; and he was forgiving even to weakness. It is, however, observable, that he treated soldiers far more kindly than officers; and among the latter, those of inferior grades, generally better than those of highest rank or of his own immediate staff.

Contrary to custom, his sympathy was bestowed most where it was most wanted: and when a man's devotion to a service is of the entire and exclusive nature of Suwarow's, we can hardly wonder to find him taxing that of others severely, and after all, seeing nothing extraordinarily meritorious in their exertions. With him, as with our heroic Nelson, the simple term "duty" was equivalent to, and exacted, the utmost devotion of which a man was capable; and it is the soul of all military organization, and the surest sign of a mind made to elevate a nation, so to identify it. No true soldier or sailor of a country ever did, or can do, more than his duty. Suwarow strove, however eccentrically, to impress this truth upon his people, and to overlay their personal vanity, by that simple and sublime abnegation of self, which has ever been the singular and majestic characteristic of those few armies that live in history, as perfect models of what armies should be.

St. Nicholas, the tutelar saint of Russia, had no more constant votary than Suwarow; but he testified his respect for every phase of Christianity alike, by asking the blessing of ministers of every sect, when he encountered them. He could, however, distinguish between the man and the function: the priest of Altorf had scarcely bestowed his benediction, when a charge being brought against him, he was sentenced to receive a dozen *coups de bâton*. A child seldom passed him but he would caress and bless it; and Duboscage mentions, that, when travelling day and night to join the army, he suddenly turned off the road towards Moscow, and arriving at his hotel at midnight, knocked, and, being admitted, stole up gently, with a light in his hand, to the bed where his children lay.

He undrew the curtains, gazed on them as they slept, whispered a blessing on them as he softly kissed their lips, and, drawing the curtain again with the greatest care, cautiously descended step by step, and throwing himself into his *kabitka*, pursued his journey. After sitting a length of time in fond and silent admiration of his daughter, the Countess Zouboff, he would start up, kiss her hand again and again, and leap about the room, thanking Heaven for the treasure it had given him. Although separated from his wife, he regarded her as a friend, and paid her all due respect. She was mistress of herself, and of his fortune. But he did wrong in marrying: his heart and soul were in his profession. War was his element, not home.

"As if increase of appetite had grown by what it fed on," his yearning after action made the consideration of his advancing age most painful to him; and, with the ingenious sophistry so common to our nature, he eagerly availed himself of any circumstance that flattered the hope he clung to, that the time when he must bid farewell to battles was still far distant. He ordered Duboscage to write a letter to Charrette, saying:—

Tell him, I admire and congratulate him. Glory to God! glory to him! Bring it this evening.

★★★★★★

Note:—That was a staple phrase in Suwarow's correspondence; ex. gr.:—Despatch to Romanzoff—
Glory to God—glory to thee;
Tourtakaye's taken, and taken by me.
Despatch to the empress—

Islawa Boga, Islawa wam!
Ismail wsjat; Suwarow tam!

Anglice:—
Glory to God—glory to thee;
Ismail is taken; Suwarow is there!

★★★★★★

Duboscage produced the epistle that goes under Suwarow's name (though no more resembling his style, than Racine's *Achille* does Homer's *Achilles*) and as he read, "such are the wishes of a soldier grown grey in the fields of honour," a very rapid undulation of the field-marshal's forehead and wrinkles was perceptible at the word "grey." It was not long after, during a conversation with a French duke, that Suwarow squeezed Duboscage's arm, and pointing to the nobleman, said, "Why, look! he has grey hairs; and, pray, have not you?"

The aversion which, from his youth, he had entertained to looking-glasses, as an unmanly piece of furniture, increased to perfect abhorrence when they began to exhibit the ravages that time was making on his person; and if he chanced to come unexpectedly upon one, he would shut his eyes, make hideous faces, and canter out of the room. To prove to those about him how little time had affected his hardihood, he frequently delivered long and somewhat unintelligible harangues to troops in the very coldest weather, and the incessant coughing and sneezing consequent on his eloquence, was perfect music to him.

Segur tells us, that, on his appointment to the rank of field-marshal, his uniform was placed on the altar of the cathedral at Warsaw, and as many chairs ranged up the aisle as there had been generals above him; when, as if to show at once what he had done and what he could do, he entered the aisle at a run, jumped over chair after chair, and having deliberately arrayed himself in his new uniform, joined most devoutly in the "*Te Deum*" that was chanted. It was on this occasion that Catherine wrote to him:—

> You know I promote no one out of his turn: I am incapable of doing any such injustice to my old officers; but it is you who have made yourself a field-marshal, by having conquered Poland.

Amongst his other whimsicalities, he entertained an idea that nothing ought to disturb a man's—and especially a soldier's—self-possession; and, in consequence, he asked the most abrupt and extrav-

35

agant questions, to try the presence of mind of strangers. According to Duboscage, he sometimes amused himself with telling fortunes, and amongst others, his (D.'s) in these words:—"Peter, son of Gabriel, no great event will agitate thy destiny: thy life will be calm and tranquil"; the fulfilment of which prediction seems to have astonished the marquis more than it is likely to do those who read his memoir.

Suwarow's extravagances were remarkable among a people with whom buffoonery was a fashion. However, it may be ridiculed, a character for eccentricity has its advantages, and is commonly allied to a degree of cunning, sagacious enough to appreciate them. There are a thousand difficulties to be removed with care and circumspection by the generality, which the eccentric man may overleap or disregard; and there is nothing incompatible with the possession of such military qualities as Suwarow's (which include no high intellectual gift) and the degree of eccentricity he associated with them.

Some, however, assume for the field-marshal a lofty position, and assert that his singularities, in their design and effect, do honour to his sagacity and perseverance. Military employment, as they contend, was his object, and he was aware how much these oddities make men known and talked of. Having neither figure nor inclination to rise by the intrigues, amatory or political, that made men great in Russia, he laboured to acquire the character of so brave and able an officer, that all would find him useful, and so eccentric a one that none would deem him dangerous. If such were his design, his success was most complete, and his contemporaries relate, that his name occurred as a natural and inevitable association, whenever a daring measure was contemplated at St. Petersburg.

Whether or not his extravagances were originally assumed from so admirable a motive, the essential excellences of his mind and character are undeniable. The impressive unity of a cathedral is the same, though the eye may rest for a moment on a grotesque corbeille, or occasionally shrink from dwelling on groups still less in keeping with the majestic ensemble of the structure. Devotion to his country's service is man's noblest duty, and never was such devotion more earnest and indefatigable than Suwarow's.

In addition to the military qualities of first-rate courage, enterprise, sagacity, *coup d'oeil,* decision, perseverance, and the master-power of stimulating to their highest stretch, these qualities in others, which gained him the imperishable fame of a practical and distinguished general who never knew defeat, Suwarow possessed, together with his ardent and irritable zeal, a degree of self-command and a self-sacrificing sense of duty, rarely found in men accustomed to command. He was a keen observer, and most accurate appreciator of men, always endeavouring to make them talk on what they were supposed to know best. His reading, both historical and military, was extensive: he spoke six languages, and read four others. However neglectful of the elegancies of life, no one was more observant of its duties. He despised wealth and disregarded pleasure; and, amid the moral and political profligacy that disgraced his country, we look in vain for a single fact that impugns the honour, the probity, the disinterestedness or the loyalty of this extraordinary man.

CHAPTER 2

Suwarow's Last Campaign

Suwarow, having; received the rank of field-marshal in the Austrian Army, and the emperor's instructions regarding his operations, quitted Vienna, after a solemn invocation of the Divine assistance in the cathedral of St. Stephen. At Villach, he overtook his countrymen, marching by an Austrian route from St. Polten, which they had left on the 12th March, doing fifty-one German miles in twenty-six days. He altered this, and they did the remaining fifty-two miles to Verona in ten. He reached Verona on the 9th April, and as its garrison defiled before him, he exclaimed, "Oh! their step is good. Victory! victory!"

At the palace prepared for him, the mirrors were ordered out, and straw was ordered in; he received the compliments of the municipality, and the blessing of the bishop, issued a stirring proclamation to the Italians, promising the protection of God and the victorious Imperial armies to the well-conducted, and a musket-ball and confiscation of property to the supporters of the French Republic; and on the morning of the 15th, set out for the Austrian headquarters near Valeggio. On meeting General Kray, he said:—

It is to you, sir, I shall owe the success I hope to meet: you have shown me the way to victory.

The seizure of Piedmont, Switzerland, and the Papal territories by the unprincipled French Government in 1798, justified, if it did not excite, the second coalition against France, of which England, Austria, Russia, Naples and Turkey, were the members; but the king of Naples, prematurely commencing hostilities, was driven from his Italian dominions, before the mightier continental powers had drawn the sword. Early in 1799, the Archduke Charles in Bavaria, Bellegarde in the Tyrol, and Kray on the Adige, with the armies under their com-

mand, amounting to near 200,000 men, awaited the arrival of Suwarow and the Russians, to march upon the French.

But the Directory, ill prepared for the struggle they had provoked,
in the hope of striking a decisive blow before the junction of the Allies, declared war in March, and pushed forward Jourdan in Germany,
Masséna in Switzerland, and Scherer in Italy, all with forces inferior
to those of their enemies. After much preliminary fighting, with various success, the republicans were defeated at Stockach in Germany, at
Feldkirch in Switzerland, and at Magnano in Italy.

When Suwarow with 22,000 Russians, reached the seat of war,
Masséna, into whose army Jourdan's had merged after its defeat, defended the Rhine from Basle to the Engadine, against the archduke
and Bellegarde; while in Italy, Scherer was falling back on the Oglio,
his troops reduced below 30,000 by their losses, and the garrisons
thrown into Mantua, Peschiera, and Brescia. A division of 6,000 men,
under Gauthier, occupied Tuscany; three times that number were scattered throughout Lombardy, Piedmont and Liguria; while the Army
of Naples under Macdonald, 30,000 strong, had received instructions
to prepare itself to march upon the Po.

On the 17th April, the first, and on the 18th, the second of two
Russian divisions, each near 10,000 strong, with six regiments of
Cossacks, joined the Austrians; and Chastelar, the chief of the staff,
proposed a reconnaissance preparatory to their advance. Suwarow
answered:—

No, no! no reconnoitring, I want no reconnoitring. It is only
useful to the timid, to tell the enemy they are coming. One
always finds the enemy when one wishes. Columns—the bayonet—the naked steel—attack—dash through! That's my reconnoitring!

Jomini says:—

An answer in which many see an empty boast, but which exhibits, more than is thought, the true genius of war.

★★★★★★

Note:—"For instance, to apply this answer to the position of the
Oglio, is it not to say in other words, 'The French are behind the
Oglio, either scattered along its course, or massed at the most
advantageous point.' Well! what matter? Let us make our main
effort on a point conforming to strategic rule, and be satisfied
with a strong demonstration on the rest of the line. If we find

the enemy scattered, the demonstration will keep him so, and the mass will crush him. If, on the contrary, we find him massed in face of our main attack, the demonstration will act on its side, and become a column of manoeuvre to take the enemy in flank. Here the decisive point is at Soncino, or at Ponterico; because, successful there, we should have turned everything posted along the saillant of the lower Oglio, and could drive it *into* the Po. It is there then that we should direct our attack, and break through the enemy."—Jomini. This note is copied for its intrinsic excellence, rather than as a paraphrase of Suwarow's words.

★★★★★★

On the 19th April, the army advanced to the Chiese, and on the 20th (Ferrara, Peschiera and Mantua being blockaded) broke up from that river; the right under Kray, advancing on Brescia, the left under Melas, on Chiari, while detached corps under Wuckassovich, towards the mountains, and Hohenzollern on the lower Oglio, threatened the flanks of Scherer's army. Kray gallantly blew open the gate, and carrying the town of Brescia, prepared to escalade its citadel; which surrendered, with a garrison of 1,200 men, on the 21st. Melas, delayed by bad roads and swollen streams, halted on the Malla. Suwarow wrote to him:—

I hear people complain that the infantry have had their feet wet. It was the fault of the weather. The march was ordered for the service of the emperor. Women, coxcombs and idlers alone require fine weather. Your chatterers who grumble at their sovereign's service, must be treated henceforth as egotists, and put out of command. Operations once resolved on, must be carried out without a moment's loss, that the enemy may not have time to recollect himself. Those who have bad health, may stay in the rear. Italy must be delivered from the yoke of Atheists and Frenchmen. Every brave officer ought to sacrifice himself to effect this. Reasoners cannot be tolerated in any army. *Coup d'oeil*, quickness and vigour are what we want just now.

Suwarow immediately pushed his headquarters beyond Brescia, his advance attacked the bridge of Pallazuolo; and Wuckassovich, descending to turn the upper Oglio by Lovere, the main body of the French fell back, and was withdrawn over the Adda. The weather had been severe, and it was the 24th April before the Allied Army had crossed the Oglio; their right moving on Bergamo, their left on Trivulgio. Hohenzollern's force entered Cremona on the following day, after some resistance. Almost simultaneously Bergamo surrendered, after a sharp encounter; and the Allies approached the Adda, in three masses, opposite Lecco, Vaprio, and Cassano; headquarters on the 25th being at Trivulgio. The siege of Peschiera and the blockade of Mantua were entrusted to General Kray, who remained behind with 20,000 men.

At this juncture Scherer had resigned to Moreau the command of the French Army, when barely numbering 28,000 men; it was stretched behind the Adda from Lecco to the Po. All the bridges had been destroyed but four. The left of the army under Serrurier, held that of Lecco; Grenier and Victor from the neighbourhood of Inzago (headquarters), supported the defenders of those of Cassano and Lodi; while the extreme right under La Boissière held Pizzighettone and the *tête-du-pont* of Gera, having detachments at Pusterlengo and Placentia. The Adda is deep and very rapid, the fall between Lecco and Trezzo (little more than twenty miles), being near 260 feet. From the lake to Cassano, the right bank commands the left, and artificial watercourses, especially in front of Cassano, add to its defensibility.

On the 26th, the Allies 50,000 strong, prepared to cross. Demonstrations were made during the day on various points; by the extreme right, on Lecco, in such strength as to lead to a serious action between the French and Russians, in which the Cossacks highly distinguished themselves on foot as *tirailleurs*, previous to the arrival of the infantry.

******

Note:—This is noticed as exhibiting these wild warriors as a more available force than we generally suppose them to be; and there is a similar and very striking instance of their effective employment, as infantry, in Varnhagen Von Ense's spirited account of Tettenborn's defeat of General Morand; the latter having 2,500 regular infantry, and Tettenborn not a soldier of that arm—all the work pertaining to it (which was far from trifling) having been gloriously carried out by these dismounted horsemen.

******

Towards evening, two central columns closely approached the river, the one near Brivio, the other some miles lower. Their orders were to establish bridges, and having passed over, to descend the stream, reinforcing themselves with the other divisions as they crossed, or turning the enemy who disputed their passage.

The left under Melas was to attack Cassano on the following morning. From Brivio to Cassano is a short march. The allied right centre surprised a passage at Brivio, repairing the ruined bridge, and driving such of Serrurier's people as they encountered, towards Lecco. The greater part of that general's division had marched with him on Vaprio, attracted there by the movements of the Allies; but hearing of the threatening aspect of affairs towards Brivio and Lecco, they countermarched, leaving a battalion at Trezzo, and the whole disposable French force was directed towards the left.

But their game was already all but lost. During the night, the allied centre, under Generals Ott and Zoph, had fixed a bridge near Trezzo, and were rapidly passing over their troops; the battalion left by Serrurier (which, trusting to the inclemency of the weather and the rapidity of the stream, had neglected its duty), being driven in confusion towards Vaprio. Here, early in the morning, Grenier's division arrived, and rallying the fugitives, vigorously attacked the Austrians; who formed to face him, with their left upon the river, covering the road which led from their bridge at Trezzo. While the affair was warmly contested, a part of Victor's division readied the ground and fell on the exposed right flank of the Allies.

A sanguinary struggle followed, and success seemed doubtful, till the numerous reinforcements successively crossing the stream, became too much for the French; and by a gallant and simultaneous advance with the bayonet, headed by the Quartermaster-General Chasteler, they were driven beyond Vaprio and Inzago; the latter village being carried by the Austrian General Ott, after a desperate hand to hand *mêlée*, in which Suwarow states that at one moment Moreau was actually taken by the allied Hussars, though subsequently rescued.

Melas had attacked the canal and entrenchments in front of Cassano at seven in the morning, and this strong ground was resolutely defended; at length the canal was passed under a heavy fire, and the advanced batteries being carried, the conflict recommenced at the *tête-du-pont* of Cassano. It was four o'clock, and great confusion was already perceptible in their rear, as fugitives and wounded came away from the Vaprio fight, before the French set fire to the bridge, and abandoned Cassano. The bridge was soon repaired; the French line, pierced on three points, fell back on Como, Milan, Melignano, and Placentia, and the allied centre and left halted for the night on the field of battle, headquarters being at Gorgonzola.

General Serrurier, finding the Allies had passed the river at Brivio in the direction of his march, and again at Trezzo in the direction he had left, became confused, and took up a position at Verderio. Next

Cassano d'Adda

day (28th) he found himself surrounded by Generals Wuckassovich and Rosenberg, and after a gallant resistance was forced to surrender, with 3,000 men. Moreau—having lost a third of his army, with the Generals Serrurier, Fressier, and Becker, twenty-two guns, and a colour—fell back on the Ticino, and Suwarow made his triumphal entry into Milan on the 29th, the tenth day only since his army broke up from the Chiese. He said to the archbishop:—

> I come to restore religion and the Pope, and to renew in the people the respect they owe to their rulers: your office should incline you to assist me.

When, in a solemn ceremony at the Duomo, this dignitary turned to Suwarow with the words "Great chief, may the Almighty bless your entrance into our city," he replied aloud in Italian "Rather pray that God may aid me to defend your temples and your monarch's throne."
To the deputies from the city he observed,—

> I am gratified by your reception: I hope the sentiments of your hearts correspond with those you have expressed"

A violent political reaction broke out at Milan, and the partisans of France owed their lives to the protection afforded them by Suwarow.
"Where shall you retire to?" he asked Serrurier at dinner.
"To Paris," he replied.
"Oh! then I shall meet you there."
"I hope so," answered the republican.
Suwarow wrote to the Emperor Francis:—

> Your Majesty's soldiers behave like heroes, and the Russians like Austrians.

And to his own sovereign:—

> Your troops never give way, and are but too happy to obey your orders in annihilating this ridiculous system of liberty and equality.

Napoleon is made to observe (in Sir W. Scott's life of him) that:

> The passage of a river is one of the most critical operations in modern war.

While he writes to the Directory:—

> *Jamais depuis que l'histoire nous retrace des opérations militaires, une*

SUWAROW CAPTURING MILAN

rivière n'a pu être un obstacle reel.

This apparent contradiction involves no real one. From the difficulty of passing a river by open force, secrecy is, or should be observed, in preparing for it; this most commonly precludes the possibility of the inferior army which has to guard its whole course, acting with effect upon any one point, before the assailant shall have established himself. But the passage of a river becomes a most critical operation, both when a general crosses it in front of his enemy's stronger mass, as Napoleon did at Aspern, and when its rapidity and localities enable the defendant to render its few available points tenable, till he can support them with his masses, as Vendôme did in his defence of this very Adda against Prince Eugene in 1705.

At each and every point where Suwarow succeeded, that illustrious leader was baffled. On the 10th August, before he could fix a bridge at Trezzo, Vendome anticipated him, and again higher up the river on the 14th. He expected, two days after, to carry Cassano, before it could be supported; but he was repulsed, and finally fell back to winter quarters on the Adige.

Some writers say that Moreau endeavoured to defend the Adda that Dessoles and Gauthier might join him from Switzerland and Tuscany; but it is known that in a previous council of war, he had already strenuously recommended a retreat on Piedmont—that Montrichard had been passed over the Po with a detachment of Scherer's army, to cooperate with Gauthier on the right of the river, and that the allied attack was simultaneous with Moreau's assumption of the command.

Whoever is responsible for it, the dissemination of 28,000 men, along a line of twenty-four leagues, rendered the defence of the Adda almost hopeless before 50,000, two-thirds of whom could have been united on any point of the ground they covered, by a single march; but the secrecy, promptitude, and energy of the Allies are not the less exemplary.

The completion of the bridge at Trezzo, in spite of difficulties which the French believed, and the Austrian pontoniers declared to be insurmountable, did them the highest honour. "*Scribentismus*" might possibly object to the determined assaults made on the strong post of Cassano, and urge that had these attacks been merely serious enough to occupy the French while the bulk of the Allied Army passed the Adda at Trezzo and Brivio, Cassano would have been won at infinitely less cost, and probably with the destruction or captivity of its defenders.

Jomini says:—

There are circumstances in which to attack an enemy on all points is to do him service; because he is thus forced to abandon posts where he would be surrounded, if he were let alone.

It is more difficult to understand why the small and beaten army of the French, hurrying from the field in three, if not four, eccentric directions, was not vigorously pursued. The case was one to which the comments of the lively Prince de Ligne are almost applicable. The prince observes:—

It will be said, as an excuse by those who have won the battle, that they are as tired as they who have lost it; that their generals are wounded. Who wants generals? Give a good horse to the first lieutenant of Croats you meet; let him cry, 'Long live Joseph II.!' and carry along with him the crowd of willing fellows whom the love of booty will bring around him. But there must be order, it will be said. There is no more need of it. It would seem there has been order, because the battle is won; and it would seem there is no longer order in the enemy's army, because the battle is lost. Supposing both out of order, the odds are surely against those who turn their backs.

But Suwarow had neither temptation nor need to profit by the prince's tactics, he having, at the Adda, near 7,000 of the finest cavalry in Europe, the greater part of whom had not drawn a sabre in the battle. Nor is this the only instance in which we have to wonder at his curious disregard of that profitable duty of a general—a vigorous pursuit of a thoroughly beaten enemy. It is, however, unquestionable that a victorious army after a battle is often in a state of momentary disorganization, which renders it more difficult than it may seem to a critic at his writing-desk, to detach a compact body of troops from the field. Even Napoleon, who, in the talent of largely profiting by success, bears the palm amongst warriors, was seldom able to pursue a beaten Russian Army with any great effect; and it may, moreover, be urged, that Suwarow's right wing was absent from the battlefield, and that the infantry of his left and centre had had hard work.

Still, he had his noble cavalry in hand; and, odd as it may sound, the conjecture forces itself upon one, that Suwarow's interest in his enemy declined the moment that enemy ceased to hold a formidable attitude, and that he almost despised the gathering in of the glorious harvest he so loved to reap. At the Trebbia and St. Gothard only do we find his practice and theory in accord on this important point.

47

Serrurier's halt at Verderio is the more unaccountable, as it was an established and admirable custom among the revolutionary generals, if at a loss for orders, to march wherever they heard the fire of cannon. He knew the Russians had crossed at Brivio; the firing must have told him that a passage was forced or contested towards Vaprio; to remain stationary was the very worst he could do.

La resolution est la première qualité dans un général. Aussi le plus mauvais parti que l'on puisse prendre à la guerre, est il presque toujours de n'en prendre aucun.—Philosophie de la Guerre.

Everything lost in war may be recovered or renewed, but time. His conduct, in this instance, recalls Buonaparte's opinion of him, given to the Directory in 1796;—

Serrurier se bat en soldat—ne prend rien sur lui—ferme—n'a pas assez bonne opinion de ses troupes—est malade.

That part of his division which maintained itself at Lecco, after occupying the Russians so as to prevent their descending the right bank of the river on the 27th, finding itself altogether cut off from the army, blew up the works it had defended, embarked on the lake and landing at Menaggio, crossed the hill to Porlezza, and rejoined Moreau on the Ticino; thus exhibiting a glorious and palpable contrast to the indecision of their general. Colonel Loyez and Captain Letort have the honour of this soldierlike proceeding. Such examples cannot be too indelibly impressed on officers of the lower ranks: disasters offer them their noblest opportunities.

The strongest body of the French Army, under Victor and La Boissière, fell back by the Pavia and Vigevano roads, on Alexandria; the troops from Lodi and Pizzighettone, under Lemoine, by Placentia on Tortona; while Moreau, with a part of Grenier's division, hurried, by Novara, to Turin, to provide for the defence of that city. He wrote to press the advance of the Army of Naples, directed Perignon to secure the passes into Liguria, and on the 7th May, having completed his arrangements, rejoined his collected little army of 20,000 men, in a masterly position behind the confluence of the Po and the Tanaro; saying, as palpably as one who "speaks though he says nothing" could do, to the numerous army of his enemy, "Come on, if you dare."

The rivers alike covered his front and flanks, the right of which rested on the citadel of Alexandria, and the left on Valenza, the centre occupying the high ground of San Salvadore. In his rear, Casale was garrisoned, and the right bank of the Po, which even to Turin commands the left, watched by small detachments. The French Army thus formed the base of a nearly equilateral triangle, of which the rivers were the sides, barely occupying four leagues from right to left. It covered the roads to Turin by Asti, and to Genoa by Acqui and Savona, and could, by a single march, have placed itself across the Po or Bormida, on the flank of an enemy threatening either Turin or Genoa.

Mr. Alison states that Suwarow, "for above a week, gave himself up to festivities at Milan;" but this is utterly at variance with the dates of his orders and his letters, by which he is shown to have resumed operations on the 1st May, on which day his headquarters were transferred to Lodi. Wuckassovich with seven battalions and cavalry, on the Novara road, covered the siege of the citadel of Milan under Lattermann; while the main army, on the 1st and 2nd May, moved in two columns to the Po, opposite to Castel San Giovanni and Placentia—head-quarters being successively at Lodi and Pasterlengo.

Suwarow's object in this movement was to have crossed the Po to fight Macdonald, and after beating him, to recross the river to Pavia, and thence march on Turin by Trino and Chivasso, leaving Tortona to be invested by Kray, when he should have taken Peschiera and Mantua; but having ascertained that Macdonald's army was still far distant, and having likewise heard from Wuckassovich that nothing hostile was in force near the Ticino, he on the 4th directed the latter officer to clear the country to the north of the Po by Vercelli and Mortara, and to push his posts to Trino and Santhia above and below Casale, and marched himself with the main army on Pavia.

Here he changed his plan and divided his force, moving Bagration's advance guard and the Austrian divisions of Zoph and Fröhlich across the Po, and directing Rosenberg with two Russian divisions, on Lomello, to threaten Valenza and communicate with Wuckassovich. Generals Ott and Klenau had been detached by Placentia, to push back Montrichard and to occupy the rich corn countries of Parma and Ferrara, communicating across the Po with Kray; who with 20,000 men besieged Peschiera and blockaded Mantua. Suwarow, accompanying the left portion of his army, was at Voghera on the 7th, and Bagration and Karacsay having blown open the gate, and carried the town of Tortona with the bayonet on the 9th (the enemy retiring to its citadel); this place became headquarters on the 10th.

Suwarow was, however, now aware of Moreau's threatening position; and on the day he entered Tortona, his troops forded the Scrivia breast high (the stream being too rapid to fix a pontoon bridge), to close upon the Bormida and Tanaro, and face their enemy. While ignorant of Moreau's intentions, and informed that Valenza was abandoned, or but slightly occupied, he had, on the 7th and 9th, instructed Rosenberg to send General Tschubaroff with four battalions, a regiment of Cossacks, and two squadrons of dragoons, to take possession of Valenza and to push his posts on Alexandria and Casale; but now these orders were necessarily countermanded, and on the 11th, Suwarow wrote to Rosenberg:—

We will leave Valenza to the future. Call in Tschubaroff; which you will have already done, if necessary. Make all haste by day and night to join us near Tortona.

Unfortunately, however, after a fruitless attempt to pass the Po on the 11th, General Tschubaroff, by swimming over his Cossacks, and seizing a ferryboat, had succeeded early in the morning of the 12th, in effecting a passage near Busignauo; and Rosenberg's zeal led him to support and follow him. They were marching on the French outposts when the order of recall arrived, and either supposing themselves too far committed to get away without a fight, or looking to success to palliate their disobedience, fell on the people before them, and the division of Grenier as it arrived to their support, with such determined energy, that they were winning rapidly; when Victor's whole division (which Moreau, apprehensive of other attacks, had for a time held back) joined in the action, and turning the Russians on both flanks, compelled them to form square and fight their way back to the river, with the loss of half their number, including General Tschubaroff killed or wounded.

Suwarow, in his order to the army of the 14th, thus bitterly comments on this transaction:—

No one can judge rightly of circumstances but upon the spot. There the hourly vicissitudes of their course can be ascertained and provided for, according to the rules of war. Report had stated that Valenza was evacuated or only weakly held. This report was false. Orders were sent to the Russian troops in that neighbourhood to unite with the army, but these orders only reached them when a portion of their advanced-guard had passed from Borgo Franco to the first island in the Po. It was not enough that these people did not immediately return, but the rest of the corps, disobeying the orders, continued the passage by a single ferry and by means of boats. Without foresight—as if bereft of reason—the battalions first over, fell upon the enemy's outposts, without considering that the troops following them could scarcely pass at the rate of a battalion in an hour and a half, &c.

After praising the gallantry of the troops, he concludes:—

Demonstrations are puerilities—generally useless, always fatiguing to the troops, and often mischievous. For the rest, a court-martial shall decide.

On hearing of the passage, Suwarow ordered it to be supported, and moved a division to make a diversion in its favour; but all was fruitless, and nothing followed these disjointed efforts, but the arrival in camp of General Förster's Russian division, and a countermand to Rosenberg, bidding him stand fast at Lomello, until the 16th; when Suwarow, reverting to his original intention of moving on Turin by the north of the Po, ordered the divisions with him to move in succession to their right, to cross that river, and Wuckassovich to threaten Casale.

A general insurrection against the French, excited by Suwarow's proclamations, now existed throughout Piedmont; and not only was Moreau's communication with France entirely interrupted by it, but his park at Asti had been vigorously attacked by a crowd of Piedmontese insurgents, calling themselves the "Christian mass." Uneasy at these circumstances, and at the perfect lull which had followed the action of the 12th on the side of the Allies, he determined to ascertain whether the latter remained in force between the Bormida and the Scrivia, or whether the route to Genoa by Novi was open to him; and accordingly, on the 16th, crossing the Bormida with 8,000 or 10,000 men, he attacked the troops at Marengo and San Giuliano as they were preparing to move towards the Po.

General Lusignan distinguished himself greatly in resisting the French, but they were gaining ground, when Bagration's force, marching from Novi in compliance with the orders issued to pass the Po, appeared upon their right flank, and with the reinforcements which the firing had brought to the Austrians from the neighbouring camp, assailed them so fiercely that they fell back in the greatest disorder to the bridge over the Bormida, with the loss of full 2,000 men. Learning nothing by this reconnaissance but the strength of his enemy on this side, finding himself seriously threatened towards Casale and Valenza, and beset on all sides by insurgents, Moreau determined on retreat.

Having despatched Victor with ten battalions to Acqui and Savona on Genoa, whence he was to join the army of Naples, he marched on the 18th May to Asti, and in twenty-four hours his advance was at Moncaglieri south of Turin, on the road thence to Liguria. Here he learned that the insurgents had gained possession of Ceva and Mondovi, both towns (the former a strong fortress) blocking up the best line of his further retreat.

An officer with four battalions was despatched to recapture them; the heavy artillery was sent to Fenestrelles with an escort of 2,000 men, who were to rejoin Moreau near Coni; while another detachment had to protect from the insurgents the interminable convoy of Italian plunder which happened at this moment to be passing into France. Mondovi was taken, but abandoned by the officer in command, on a report that the Austrians were approaching. Grouchy superseded him, and again took Mondovi, but failed in all his efforts to recover Ceva; into which an Austrian detachment from Tortona, under Captain Schmelzer, had thrown itself and maintained it gallantly.

In this perplexity Moreau, who had marched on Coni and provided for its defence, unwilling to retire by the Col di Tende, and yet desirous to keep his field artillery with him, ordered a reconnaissance of the mountains towards Garessio, to see if a way could be made there, so as to turn Ceva and regain the highroad beyond it. All the reports declared the impracticability of cutting a passage for artillery, except that of the *aide-de-camp*, Guilleminot, which pronounced that 2,000 workmen would effect it in three days.

The road was made—the army working day and night, and on the 7th June, every gun and man, passing by Garessio and Ormea, were safe in Liguria, in spite of the "Christian mass" on one side the mountains, and the insurgents of Oneglia on the other. Casale had already been carried by Wuckassovich, when Moreau's retreat, delivering Valenza to the Allies, they occupied it, and on the 21st entered Alexandria and blockaded its citadel. The divisions on the south of the Po continued to cross that river after the action of the 16th, and the army moved in two columns on Turin.

Owing to the weather and the swollen streams, it was the 26th before the army approached the city, and on the following day the excited people rose upon the French and opened the gates to the Allies, who speedily drove the enemy into the citadel, which was immediately invested. Above 300 pieces of artillery, with immense supplies of all kinds were found in Turin, where 4,000 Piedmontese soldiers abandoned the republican colours and joined Count Latour, to whom Suwarow had entrusted the reorganisation of their army.

★★★★★★

Note:—Though the barefaced brigandage and impudent fallacies of French rule and fraternity in Italy had prepared its people for the general rising, which, from Calabria to the Alps, occurred on the appearance of the Allies, the energetic insurrection in Piedmont was more immediately due to Suwarow's proclamations, promising the restoration of their monarch and their former government. In fulfilment of this promise, and for the interest of the common cause, he immediately proceeded to reorganise the Piedmontese Army and militia, by which the Allies would have gained an accession of 30,000 good troops, and a local force equal to the duties of the country. But Austrian policy at once put a stop to this.

On the 17th May, the Emperor Francis expressed to him his entire disapprobation of his proceedings; declaring he would admit of no government but his own in the conquered countries, which he would send a Civil Commissioner to administrate, and forbidding the reorganisation of the Piedmontese Army; directing instead that some battalions of Piedmontese light troops should be raised for his service. The result of this selfish and, to the general cause, suicidal policy, is detailed in one of the last letters Suwarow wrote before leaving Italy; striving then as ever, in spite of the unworthy treatment he had received, to realise whatever could forward the general cause:—

September 1st, 1799.

To the Emperor Francis,

Having constantly before me the great aim of the united Cabinets to secure the conquests made in Italy, I consider it my duty to submit the following statement to Your Imperial Majesty. For the last three months we have been doing our utmost to form light battalions of Piedmontese soldiers for Your Majesty, but all we have been able to effect is, in some degree, to strengthen the regiment, Belgioioso; and to form on paper a battalion out of the *Jäger* corps, Brentano; and the light battalion *Bona Casa;* as the men who enter, desert daily in such numbers that scarcely any remain. Thousands of these deserters, hungry and penniless, infest the country, and there are full 10,000 of them in Turin. The cause of the disinclination of the Piedmontese to remain in the service, is to be found in their devotion to their own of-

53

ficers, and the hostile feeling of the latter towards us, now they are removed from the service.

Under these circumstances, I see no way of employing these destitute, idle, and desperate men for the public good, but by the reformation of the Piedmontese regiments and corps under their former officers, which could be effected in a week. These troops could be disseminated in brigades or regiments through the Imperial Army, and thus powerfully reinforce it. Their local knowledge would be invaluable in the approaching mountain operations. Be pleased to consider this respectful proposal, which may be right or may be wrong, and communicate Your Majesty's decision.

Suwarow.

★★★★★★

Columns were directed up the Alpine passes on Pignerol, Susa, Fenestrelles, and Aosta; the two former posts were carried, and Bagration's dragoons pursued fugitives to the frontiers of Dauphiné; a hundred pieces of field artillery and sixty mountain guns were sent to Valenza, where an entrenched camp was formed. Peschiera had surrendered on the 7th, and Pizzighettone on the 10th; Ferrara, Ravenna, and the citadel of Milan had since fallen into the hands of the Allies. General Ott had seized the pass of Pontremoli and pushed his posts to Sarzana and Massa, on the road between Genoa and Tuscany; and on the 30th May, Bellegarde descending from the Engadine had reached Chiavenna with a reinforcement of 17,000 Austrians.

The capture of the city of Turin, a ten days' labour completed in a month, seems all connected with these operations; on which even flatterers could have congratulated Suwarow. Moreau's weak and beaten army falling back from the Adda on diverging roads, was not followed in its retreat on Alexandria and Turin, and the insurgents alone impeded or harassed either its march to Moncaglieri or its subsequent operations of a fortnight's duration previous to its descent upon Liguria.

★★★★★★

Note:—Schmelzer's detachment of 250 men moving through the mountains on the 19th and 20th May, by Acqui and Spigno, on Ceva, passed near both Victor's and Grouchy's people, and may thus account for the erroneous statement in the *Victoires et Conquêtes*, that after Moreau's repulse on the 16th, Bagration and Karacsay returned towards Novi and Acqui. These generals and their troops having both moved with the army to the north of the Po, Wuckassovich was the first and only general of the Allies that came near Moreau's army in its retreat on Liguria; his advance guard from Moncaglieri, and Mondovi reaching Ceva on the evening of the 2nd June, on the morning of which day the last French posts had withdrawn from before it.

★★★★★★

On leaving Milan on the 1st May, Suwarow in the plan of operations signed by his quartermaster-general, declares his intention:—

Of beating the French force advancing from Naples, Rome, and Tuscany, to the help of the enemy in Piedmont, before their junction, and then to move by Pavia and the left of the Po on Turin.

And in accordance with this just design, we find him at Pasterlengo on the 4th (having ascertained that Macdonald's army was still far distant), ordering the march of the army on Pavia. But here he changed his views, and, apparently supposing Moreau too weak to interfere with him, and hoping to secure Tortona if not Alexandria, before advancing on Turin, divided his army, and proceeded himself with the greater portion of it across the Po, to beleaguer Tortona and point on Genoa; till, roused by the threatening attitude assumed by Moreau at San Salvadore, his instinct of direct attack led him to concentrate upon his front, as closely as the intervening streams of the Bormida and Tanaro would let him.

Here, separated by the swollen Po, and beyond the reach of mutual support, the two great divisions of his army were held in check by Moreau's inferior force, while Suwarow vacillated: first angrily ordering Rosenberg to join him, then countermanding his order, till at length, overcoming his reluctance to show himself baffled, he readopted his original idea of marching on Turin by the left of the Po, recklessly leaving his antagonist to march on Genoa and unite with Macdonald if he chose.

★★★★★★

Note:—Accident and numbers saved Suwarow from the usual consequences of such chivalrous generalship. Tempelhoff tells us that:—

The Duke of Brunswick allowed Kellermann to join Dumouriez, that he might fight one battle instead of two, and accordingly His Highness fought only one; it was that of Valmy, which sent him out of France.

One of our poets says well:—

Discretion and hardy valour are the twins of honour, and reared together make a conqueror;—divided, but a talker.

Of all errors in war, none is so hazardous (and, wonderful to say, none so frequent) as a gratuitous dissemination or separation of a force before it has struck its "swashing blow;" unless it be a voluntary disregard of an opportunity to crush an important portion of a hostile force, before it shall unite with another kindred army.

★★★★★★

In carrying out this operation, Suwarow's headquarters were on the 21st at Candia; where, had he adhered to his original intention, they would have been at latest, on the preceding 7th! Which result, at a period when, whether as regarded Moreau's or Macdonald's proceedings, time was invaluable to his antagonists, flagrantly exposes the emptiness of his dogma—"No rule and line work: *coup d'oeil*," compared to the simple strategic rule of adopting the most advantageous measure, and allowing no secondary object to divert you from it. From the Adda to Turin is seven marches, and a direct move on it would not only at once have given that city to Suwarow, but have forced Moreau with greater or less loss, to have saved himself in Liguria, or perhaps even in France.

With so plain and so easily attainable an object before him, and which his own sagacious common sense had already adopted, we seek in vain (even in Suwarow's own correspondence) for any palliating answer to the archduke's biting but natural query: "by what inconsistency did he march on Tortona, to change his mind again a fortnight after?" The fact is palpable that Suwarow, having clearly seen and at once adopted what was most advantageous, allowed himself to be diverted from it by secondary and uncertain advantages—an error as detrimental in its consequences as any slowness and want of energy, in the methodical generals he despised.

When in ridiculing the maxim of "*slow and sure*," he affirmed that "the slow in war can only be sure of paying more dearly than they need, for all they gain" it might have occurred to him that the general who loses sight of a primary object, for a secondary one, is in a precisely similar predicament; and that measures which gain nothing or little, are as completely nullified in war by grand results, as absolutely in action. The man who walks ever so quickly on a wrong road, may be longer in reaching his object, than he who goes even slowly towards it by a more direct route; besides that he will do his work at a greater cost of wear and tear, fatigue and trouble, and be by so much less capable of pursuing ulterior objects. This was unquestionably the case in Suwarow's movement from Milan to Turin.

In the operations now referred to, Moreau shone a consummate leader; sustaining to a noble tone, the morale of a beaten army, scarce a third the strength of his adversary's; and in a week after its defeat and apparent dispersion (having, meantime, himself provided for the defence of Turin), fixing it in a position so justly studied, that in it, for ten days, he paralyzed the overwhelming force which threatened him, and severely punished the only portion of it that attempted to assail him.

His able and honest brother-soldier St. Cyr, characterizes the reconnaissance of the 16th on San Guiliano as imprudent and rash, likening it to Rosenberg's affair of the 12th at Basignano, and saying that good luck on both sides alone saved the leaders from the signal punishment they respectively so well deserved. But surely this is hypercriticism as regards Moreau. Never was reconnaissance more fully justified by the importance of its object: that of ascertaining if the route to Genoa by Novi were open to his army; nor could any reconnaissance ascertain this, but one made in strength and well pushed out.

Had accident deferred it for a single day, the full success that would have crowned it, might have changed the fortune of the campaign; but, through one of those cross purposes that mock the best designs of the ablest players in the game of war, at the very moment that Suwarow, baffled by Moreau's skill and boldness, was leaving the Novi road to Genoa open to him, the repulse of his reconnaissance by the troops crossing his front to move out of his way, convinced him that it was hopelessly closed against him, and that he had nothing for it but to gain the Ligurian territory through insurgent Piedmont.

And how nobly he did this! What chivalrous self-forgetfulness seems to characterize his proceedings! What *preux* knight ever shone more brilliantly generous and daring than Moreau appears, in sending his efficient infantry under Victor to reinforce Macdonald, and then plunging with his little band, amid countless insurgents liable at any moment to be joined by an army six-fold his strength, to preserve to his country the guns she had confided to more favoured chiefs, and the discreditable trophies which, for a season, raised their fame above his own honest and well-earned reputation.

Nor was this done at any sacrifice of duty as a prudent chief. His one rapid march on Moncaglieri, at once placed his army on the double line of retreat by Mondovi and the Col di Tende, and all he afterwards did, was executed in comparative security. However, threatened by overwhelming numbers, even had he failed in turning Ceva and passing by Garissio, a retreat by Coni and the Col di Tende was open to him as a certain last resource.

His grand merit was in not having allowed himself to be deterred from what he desired to do, by the idea that his enemies might have prevented him had they chosen; and though it taxes our credulity too strongly to assume, as Jomini does, that his object was to decoy the Allies from Macdonald who was far away, by bringing their numerous force upon his little band, with which they were almost in contact,—more especially when we consider that one of his prime objects was the protection of the vast convoys moving to France by the Col di Tende and Mont Cenis,—it cannot be doubted that he was prepared fearlessly to meet the worst they could have done, after he had placed himself on his new line of retreat.

Luckily the Allied Army did not pursue him, and the opposition and obstacles he encountered, were attended with no worse effect than that of procrastinating his and Macdonald's junction. It was, however, on this junction previous to a battle, that the cause of France in Italy depended; and it may be observed that nothing could have prevented its being thus effected, had Moreau thought it expedient to have left his heavy material at Alexandria, and to have marched on Genoa by Acqui and Savona, as Victor did—arriving there on the 22nd May. He, however, deemed it fittest to adopt the more hazardous line and the arduous duties associated with it, and he triumphantly surmounted its various and perplexing difficulties, with a calm, an enterprising, and a heroic spirit which every soldier must delight to honour.

In the last week of May, Macdonald's army reached Tuscany, and together with the troops who held that province and Bologna, comprised a force of near 35,000 men. His left, on the 30th, easily carried Pontremoli and effected a junction with Victor's division, which had marched from Genoa to the head of the Val di Taro. Having refreshed his troops and received Moreau's assurance that he would join him with his army, if not by Pontremoli, by the Bochetta and Novi, Macdonald on the 9th June moved on Modena—two divisions of his army advancing by Bologna, and three descending the passes of the Apennines by both banks of the Secchia. Victor's division remained in the mountains till the main body should approach Parma.

Five thousand Austrians of Kray's army under Hohenzollern held

Modena, between which city and Bologna, Klenau stood with 4,000 men, to cover the passage of the Panaro. Forty miles west of Modena, Ott with his division, composing Bellegarde's advance, occupied Fornovo and observed the valleys of the Taro and Trebbia; with orders from Suwarow to avoid all needless fighting, but should it be unavoidable, to do it with the naked steel: all experience showing that the enemy could not stand that fighting. As the ridge of the Apennines runs parallel to the high road from Modena to Parma, and its lateral valleys descend upon it at right angles, these detachments were perilously placed; no delusion could possibly have supposed that these corps were capable of throwing back Macdonald; and the childish futility of their position is most evident, when we reflect that, even if they could have done so, their success would only have forced him to do exactly what he ought to have done: *i e.*, to have united with Moreau behind the Apennines by Sarzana and Sestri.

Kray, who commanded on this side, was on the left of the Po with 10,000 men, whom he had drawn from the force blockading; Mantua. The position of these bodies illustrates the Austrian system of war, in which armies are parcelled out and exposed to ruin, to do the duty of a brigade of cavalry. On the 10th and 11th, there was skirmishing before Modena, but on the 12th, the Austrians there were attacked at once from Bologna and the mountains, and completely overpowered. The wreck of Hohenzollern's corps escaped on Mirandola; indebted for the power of doing so to Klenau, who vigorously opposed the French right, and prevented their passage over the Panaro, and consequent seizure of the Mirandola road, till hearing of Hohenzollern's disaster, he fell back on Ferrara. Macdonald, who was wounded in this affair, continued his advance, and entered Parma on the 14th; Victor descended the Val di Taro, and General Ott retired upon Placentia; whence, having garrisoned the citadel and destroyed the bridge, he was driven on the 16th, and hotly pursued over the Tidone.

On Macdonald's advance, Suwarow, with 30,000 men, besieged the citadel of Turin; 7,000, under Schweikowsky and Seckendorf, blockaded Tortona and Alexandria; Bellegarde was at Pavia with 15,000. Kray's blockading army and detachments to 38,000 men, and full two-thirds of that number under Fröhlich, Lusignan, Wuckassovich, and Haddik, observed passes and carried on operations against the enemy in the Alps and Apennines; while more than 20,000 insurgent Italians, some armed and the rest desirous of being so, had attached themselves to different bodies of the army. This dissemination of such

RUSSIANS CROSSING THE ALPS

an army, however faulty, was in no way dangerous, while Moreau's 25,000 men were extended 100 miles, from Bardinetto to the Val di Taro. (Jomini says:—"*Ainsi le Maréchal forcé d'obtempérer aux ordres du Conseil Aulique, avait tellement éparpillé ses forces,*" &c.)

But on the 10th June, under the impression that Macdonald's army had already joined that of Moreau, by Sestri and the Corniche road, Suwarow prepared to concentrate his forces, and wrote to Kray:—

> The enemy intends to move with his collected force from Genoa on Alexandria and Milan. Your Excellency well knows what may result from this. Your known success in war, your experience and activity, of which you gave so striking an example at Verona, make me desire, my dear and brave friend, to have you by my side in the battle we are about to fight; which will probably decide the fate of Italy. I beg Your Excellency to come as soon as possible to Alexandria. Let every disposable regiment of infantry and cavalry move with all despatch. I hope, with the aid of God and such troops, to beat the enemy. It will be a pleasure to me, my true friend, to owe to you a part of this victory. You will leave the command of the blockade of Mantua to Lieut.-Colonel Dano.

Kray did not comply with this pressing and persuasive invitation. He had received an autographic order from the Emperor Francis, to act independently of Suwarow, till Mantua had fallen; and, in consequence, he had posted Klenau and Hohenzollern as described; he now sent three battalions and six squadrons to join Suwarow, and remained with the rest of his troops near Mantua. All was, however, bustle in Piedmont: engineers were despatched from Turin to strengthen Valenza and Pavia, guns were sent to the *têtes-de-pont* and fieldworks, the fortresses were ordered to be provisioned for three months, detached corps hastened in from all sides to Turin; and on the 11th June Suwarow marched from that city to Asti with the Russian battalions, leaving General Kaim, with twelve battalions and cavalry, to besiege the citadel and watch the Alpine passes.

On the 13th, at Alexandria, Suwarow first received certain news of the fact and direction of Macdonald's advance; on which he reiterated his orders to Ott, "to avoid all engagements till the arrival of the army;" directed Bellegarde to call in all his detachments, and to take post under Alexandria, on the left of the Bormida, occupying its *tête-de-pont*, and leaving only cavalry posts across the river; wrote to Kray to reinforce Ott or Hohenzollern, to send all he could to meet the enemy; and in two successive orders, impressed upon the troops his expectations and their duties.

The enemy's army must be put to flight, with the cold steel— bayonets, sabres, and pikes. It is 27,000 strong, of which 7,000 only are French soldiers, the rest a mob of conscripts. The artillery to fire as it sees occasion; it need not confine itself to the line. The cavalry and Cossacks must fall on the enemy's flanks. In the attack, there must be no hesitation; nor, when the enemy is beaten, must he have time given him to get into order. If he surrender, he must be spared, and told to throw down his arms. All the troops in the attack are to call out "surrender," and the Cossacks, as they charge, will cry, *"balesarm*—pardon—*jettele-sarm."* (Suwarow's mode of spelling *"A bas les armes—Jettez les armes."*) The cavalry must raise this cry as they charge home, and dash headlong on the batteries, which is their particular duty. The Cossacks must destroy the bridges in rear of the enemy, and thus reduce him to despair.

All must be merciful to the prisoners. Everyone must do his utmost; and without any consideration of fatigue, the enemy must be followed night and day, till he is destroyed. In the attack, the drums will roll and the soldiers cheer. The music must play while the battle goes on, and in the pursuit, while the cavalry are cutting and slashing, that they may hear it. The Cossacks will know the generals by their staff, and will cry "pardon" to them; and if they don't surrender cut them down. On reaching the enemy, the kettles, &c., must not be sent too far to the rear, that the cooking may go on immediately on his defeat; but the conquerors must also have bread in their haversacks and water in their canteens. The cavalry must forage for themselves.

The state of the roads greatly delayed the pontoons, which had to be carried to the river by hand, and it was late on the 15th before the Bormida bridge was laid, and the troops began to pass. The Austrian division of Fröhlich, and what remained of Ott's, in the left column; twenty Russian battalions, under Rosenberg and Förster, in the right; thirty squadrons of cavalry, with Cossacks; a sufficient artillery and a pontoon train with each column; composed this perfectly efficient force of about 30,000 men. As it, was crossing the Scrivia, news came that Moreau's people were showing themselves on the descending slopes of the Bochetta; but Suwarow was not now, with an enemy's army as his object, to be deluded from it by any secondary motives. He bade Alcaini blow up the works of the town of Tortona and join Bellegarde with his blockading force, as soon as the rear-guard of the army had passed him; and to Bellegarde himself he wrote:—

It is not possible to halt the army now; concentrate all you have except your observation posts on Alexandria and the other side of the Bormida; if you cannot continue the blockade of Alexandria, fall back on Valenza, but that you must defend.

On the same day (16th June) he writes to Kaim:—

My dear Kaim, I am off to Placentia to beat Macdonald; make haste and take the citadel, or I shall sing *Te Deum* before you.

At noon on the 17th, the Allied Army approached the Tidone—near fifty miles from the Bormida—where they found Ott's corps falling back in great disorder. Chasteler, with the advance, supported him; but the French, who had three divisions present, still pressed onward; their cavalry charging up the high road, carried a battery of eight pieces, and Dombrowsky's Poles, upon their left, pushed back the force opposed to them; when Suwarow directed four Russian battalions to charge with the bayonet on their front, and two corps of Cossacks with their levelled pikes upon their left flank. This broke them bodily, and they fled in disorder; leaving the French right wing uncovered, to be charged in front and flank with similar impetuosity and success.

The republicans fought bravely, and a part of their infantry halted in squares; but the increasing numbers of the Allies, and their reiterated attacks with the bayonet, were too much for them. The whole force was broken, and those who escaped were chiefly indebted for their safety to the numerous ditches and water courses which impeded the pursuing horsemen. These latter halted on the Tidone.

This river, with the Trebbia and Nura, runs from south to north across the field of the approaching conflict, into the Po, the course of which is from west to east. Placentia is on the Po, a short league east of the right bank of the Trebbia; in front of which river the French Army, of upwards of 30,000 men, was posted, its right occupying the village of San Nicolo, its left that of Castellegio. The hostile armies were very nearly of equal strength, but that of the Allies received slight augmentations during the battle, to facilitate the junction of which they had thrown a bridge across the Po. A small detached corps, under General

Wellesky, covered the right of their army towards Bobbio.

In addition to Suwarow's general order of battle, already given, the particular directions for the 18th June were, that the three attacking columns should march upon the Nura; the right, under Rosenberg, by Castellegio, Settimo, and Caselle; the centre, under Förster, by Grignano and Valera; the third and left, under Melas, by the high road to Placentia, passing to the right of that city, and reinforcing himself with the garrison of its citadel. The advance to be in a direct successive *échelon* from the right; each column improving the success obtained by its preceding one, and turning the enemy upon the Nura and the Po, from the mountains and their expected reinforcements.

The cavalry were directed to attack in two chequered lines, with squadron intervals, so that the second line, if necessary, could come into, or pass through those of the first. The enemy's flanks and the bridges in his rear were again pointed out as the special objects of their exertions, and mercy was again enjoined, whenever the enemy should cry "pardon." The infantry were desired to fire as little as possible, but to push on with the bayonet and make prisoners. All were directed to forget that such a word as "halt" existed. "We are not now going to a drill ground," are the words of this earnest soldier; "the only battle words are—forward—dash on—the sabre—the bayonet—hurrah, boys!" and the pursuit was directed to be headlong, that the defeated enemy might be utterly annihilated.

The parole issued was Theresa—the countersign Kolin—the 18th being the anniversary of that famous Austrian victory. At ten o'clock a discharge of artillery gave the signal to advance, and every band struck up some martial air, as the directing wing of this gallant army stepped off exultingly to battle. It was near two o'clock when the French opened their fire on the approaching columns, the right of which impetuously attacked the Polish legion. Victor's division, and successive reinforcements from the French centre, obstinately but vainly opposed the Russians; and after an enormous loss, the French left wing was entirely thrown over the Trebbia and pursued by the Russians, till the darkness of night obliged them to halt at Settimo—a league beyond the river.

The fighting in the centre was lukewarm. The French had weakened theirs to support their left, and General Melas, under some apprehension for the Tortona high road on the allied left, had withdrawn so large a force to that direction, from the centre, that the remainder were unable to improve or second Rosenberg's success. This misdirected reinforcement found General Ott combatting successfully the

French right; which, with its aid, he was enabled to drive in great confusion over the Trebbia. At night the French centre also withdrew over the river, and a heavy cannonade appeared to have closed the battle.

The arms had been piled, and the tired men were sleeping, when confused sounds from the French position attracted the attention of the allied outposts; and their patrols, on entering the bed of the river, saw dark masses moving rapidly towards them. The cry "to arms" and the opening fire, awoke the men, who rushed tumultuously, horse and foot, down to the stream, while the artillery on both sides opened, and a sanguinary *mêlée* took place in the river's bed by moonlight. The French at length withdrew, and the Trebbia again separated the combatants; except where Rosenberg and his brave men passed the night in square by Settimo, whence, at daybreak, finding themselves unsupported, they marched back to their comrades across the river.

Suwarow, having repeated his preceding orders for the next day's battle, and particularly commanded Melas not to move his reserve to the left, wrapt himself in his cloak and slept among his soldiers. In the morning Kray's detachment and two battalions from Valenza joined the Allies, who were preparing to advance, when a cloud of light troops passed the river along the whole line, while heavy columns appeared to threaten their right, in front and flank. Bagration, with the extreme right, was marched at once against the outflanking body composed of Dombrowsky's legion, and attacking them with vigour, drove them back, capturing both guns and colours. The absence of his troops, however, enabled Victor and Rusca's divisions to make a serious impression on the right of Schweikowsky's troops, driving them back, and surrounding the regiment of Rosenberg, which extricated itself with distinguished intrepidity.

★★★★★★

Note:—Most troops disperse when broken; the Russians always mass themselves. They owe this admirable point of discipline in some degree, to the Turks, whose numerous cavalry being paid for heads, decapitate fugitives; so that though resistance may be dangerous, flight is certain death.

★★★★★★

A part of the reserve checked the enemy, till Bagration, returning from the repulse of Dombrowsky, appeared upon his flank, when a simultaneous attack obliged the republicans to fall back on the Trebbia, where they maintained themselves. The French centre advanced in two columns, the right composed of Olivier's division, the left of

Suwarow at Trebbia

Montrichard's. This latter had scarcely passed the Trebbia, when its leading regiment, attacked in front by the Russian infantry under Förster, and seeing the Austrian cavalry on its flank, was seized with a panic and fled; communicating fear and disorder to the whole division, which was driven in frightful confusion across the river. The Austrian cavalry, recalled by Melas to the left, hurried to a second charge on the exposed flank of Olivier's division, which was also driven beyond the Trebbia. The French right had been directed to move round the left flank of the Allies on the Tidone, and having done so, found itself compromised, and fought its way back again with difficulty and loss.

Suwarow was anxious to continue the battle during the night, but his troops were quite exhausted, and the attack was delayed until four o'clock on the following morning. At that hour they advanced, and were quickening their march on finding the French fires abandoned, when an intercepted letter from Macdonald to Perignon exposed to Suwarow the state of the enemy's army, and the direction of its retreat.

Macdonald had lost 12,000 men and nearly all his generals, his cavalry was half destroyed, his artillery unserviceable, and his ammunition almost expended. Under these circumstances, hearing nothing of Moreau or Lapoye, knowing his enemy was receiving reinforcements, and that Parma, Reggio, and Modena, in his rear, were already occupied by the Austrians, he determined to fall back.

★★★★★★

Note:—This officer, Lapoye, despatched from Liguria with 2,500 to join Macdonald by the Val di Trebbia, was at Bobbio on the 16th; it was, however, the 20th before he appeared on the flank of the Allies, when Wellesky's detachment drove him to the mountains, with considerable loss.

★★★★★★

The allied columns were directed to hurry the pursuit, and Suwarow accompanying that of the right, overtook Victor's division at the Nura, attacked it in front and flank, and completely dispersed it, obliging the 17th demi-brigade to lay down its arms. Melas, on the left, contenting himself with the capture of the French wounded at Placentia, including Generals Olivier, Rusca, Talm, and Cambray, and above 7,000 men and officers, despatched a single division after the enemy who repulsed it at the Nura. Next day the army reached the Larda, where Suwarow halted on the 22nd, heard of Bellegarde's defeat by Moreau, and facing about on the following day to meet him, entrusted the further pursuit of Macdonald to General Ott. He wrote to the Emperor Francis:—

> Captain Torres can inform Your Majesty of the glorious and celebrated events that have occurred. The enemy made wonderful exertions, but the heroism of the Allies surpassed them. As to me, my only merit is that of having fulfilled Your Majesty's commands. You directed me to attack the enemy and deliver Italy. The enemy is vanquished and Italy is free.

It is said, that in the course of these operations, finding a corps of Austrian cavalry waiting on the bank of one of the rivers for pontoons, he gave them a practical reproof, by ordering up a regiment of Cossacks, and coolly placing himself at their head, swam the stream. On the 23rd and 24th, he made forced marches to reach Moreau, who had debouched from the Bocchetta with 14,000 men, occupied Gavi on the 16th, and Novi on the 18th, and subsequently (having first raised the blockade of Tortona) defeated Bellegarde on the 20th near San Giuliano, with a loss of 2,500 men; this general having left the strong position assigned to him by Suwarow, to cross the Bormida, and court a collision to which his force was in all respects unequal.

The reason given by him for having done this, was that the ground on the right of the river was good for cavalry action, and that he feared Moreau would embarrass Suwarow, if he did not engage him. After his defeat, however, having resumed his position on the left of the Bormida, he found Moreau equally unwilling to leave him in it, or to attack it; and after a vacillation very like Suwarow's, when he (Moreau) occupied the ground in question, and a loss of four days at this interesting period, Moreau (having revictualled the citadel of Tortona) fell back on the 25th, on which day Suwarow reached the Scrivia.

On the 27th, the Allied Army encamped on the Orba, and Moreau's resumed its position on the Bocchetta. Suwarow had written to Bellegarde on the 22nd from Firenzuola:—

> Tomorrow I march from this. On the 25th without fail I will be at Castel Nuovo di Scrivia. Haddick will have reinforced you with twelve battalions, so that if the enemy will stay, we shall have him about San Giuliano or Bosco, between our two fires. This is our game. I depend on you:—you trust in me, and we will serve Moreau as we have served Macdonald.

The latter, after fighting his way through Hohenzollern's and Klenau's corps, which had re-occupied his line of retreat, and repulsing the troops that pursued him, reached Tuscany and proceeded thence by the Sarzana and Sestri road to Genoa, which he reached on the 17th July: Victor having already arrived there by Pontremoli. The citadel of Turin had surrendered on the 20th June to General Kaim, who found in it vast supplies of arms and ammunition, and upwards of 600 pieces of artillery.

Suwarow deserved to conquer on the Trebbia! The concentration of his army as he marched on Macdonald, the orders left with Belle-garde for his conduct and the security of the general communications, the direction and the perseverance of his attacks, and the rapidity of his return upon Moreau, are alike admirable. If Melas had obeyed his orders, the victory of the 18th would have been complete; and had Kray joined him with half the men he uselessly retained on the left of the Po, or of those more than uselessly employed on its right, Mac-donald could hardly have escaped complete destruction. As it was, full half his army was put *hors de combat*, the prisoners alone amounting to 4 generals, 506 officers, and 12,778 men.

How little the disposition and dispersion of the men at Modena and Ferrara was expected by Suwarow appears from his letter of 11th June to Bellegarde:—

> Count Hohenzollern who commands Kray's advance, will leave four squadrons, a battalion, and a detachment of *chasseurs* at Fornovo, and send Your Excellency the six battalions and chasseurs that remain, by forced marches.

There is not a more spotless wreath of glory than that won by Suwarow on this occasion. The junction of his antagonists failed, from Moreau's determination to attempt it by the Bocchetta. The reason given by him for taking this road, occupied in force by his enemies, instead of others that were perfectly open, is, "that it is eight marches from Genoa to Parma by Pontremoli, and that he could not move by the 9th June." Had he moved on the 10th with such part of his army as had arrived at Genoa, to be followed by the rest, he would have been at Parma on the 17th by Pontremoli, or on the 15th by Val di Taro. (From Genoa to Parma, by Pontremoli, is 130 miles; by the Val di Taro, 80. Neither road was at that time practicable for artillery.) Macdonald leaving Tuscany on the 9th, was six marches from that city, and his route was occupied by 15,000 Austrians.

All Suwarow's promptitude could not have brought him to Parma before the 19th June; and his letter, as well as common sense, proclaims that he would not have dreamt of marching eastward till he was assured, by Macdonald's descent from the Apennines, that he did not intend (as Suwarow and the Austrian cabinet alike expected) to join Moreau by Sestri, and debouch with their united armies from the Bocchetta, A delay of four days in Macdonald's advance—if not less—would have assured the junction. In the measure adopted, a junction previous to a battle was next to impossible. Macdonald had to march near two hundred miles to Tortona (where the junction was to be effected) whereas not one of the 100,000 Allies, except the corps before him, was half that distance from it.

Moreau writes—erroneously indeed—as early as the 7th of June, "that the enemy were sending all they could towards Parma," supposing Macdonald, by forced marches of a week, upon the Trebbia. As he was, he could not have moved without the knowledge of the corps in his front; and the Allies had 60,000 men not three marches from it, and 30,000 men more, not six. How could a junction be expected without a battle, when Tortona is still 40 miles from the Trebbia? And yet the object of the French was to unite before they fought!

It was not three years before this event, that the junction of Davidovich and Alvinzi failed, from the former attempting to force a passage between the Adige and the lake of Garda, when the road down the valley of the Brenta was entirely open to him; and this short sketch will furnish another instance of a similarly hazardous experiment. When Moreau had descended on Gavi on the 16th, his weakness caused him to be so circumspect that he did not leave Novi (two leagues from Gavi) till the 19th; and then to be diverted from the one great object of his movement.

Our sympathies are all in favour of Macdonald, for he was brave, unfortunate, and slandered; but doubtless he erred in neglecting Moreau's wise precaution to keep near the mountains, and in extending his army on the 19th to turn both flanks of an enemy who acted in masses and had already proved too strong for him. Still his resolution to attack, as well as his original idea of seizing a bridge over the Po, liberating the garrison of Mantua, and cutting Kray's force to pieces, to fight Suwarow afterwards on the line of his communications, were just and energetic conceptions; while his determined resistance, to give Moreau time to join, and his lion-like retreat, demand our highest praise. The ungenerous reproaches of his rulers have been repeated by Jomini, with reflections of his own, calculated to justify and perpetuate them. The baron is doubtless "a man having authority," but it is hoped the annexed note will show that in this case, at least, his censure has no right to become history.

★★★★★★

He says, (chap. 87, *Wars of the Revolution*):—

Prudence required that Macdonald should act quickly; nevertheless, from motives unknown to us, he remained ten days in complete inaction, and certainly half that time was enough to rest his army and concert his operations with Moreau.

And again:—

If the reproach of staying too long at Naples be unfounded, it will be more difficult to refute that of having debouched too slowly from Tuscany.

In the correspondence of Moreau and Macdonald, as given in the *Précis des évènemens Militaires*, we find the former writing from Alexandria on the 16th May, that:—

He is about to retire on Coni, but that he will join Macdonald as soon as possible by Genoa.

Macdonald on the 19th May, from Montefiascone, expressly states that five or six days is the time he requires to refresh his army, and afterwards from Lucca, that he is ready to march to Moreau, either by the Corniche or Modena road, but that he should prefer the latter. A despatch from Dessoles, (Moreau's *chef d'état major*) dated Genoa, May 23, mentions that Moreau is near Coni, but that all communication with him is cut off by the insurgents, and continues:—

Victor, who arrived here yesterday, will first operate his junction with you, and according to what he told me, General Moreau, after putting his artillery in safety, will march to join you by Genoa. Without knowing General Moreau's dispositions, it strikes me that, at present, it is your business to wait, especially if the junction of Victor is not sufficient to ensure you success, for, if the enemy manoeuvres, your position will force you to offer battle with inferior forces.

The next communication is from Moreau, dated Genoa, June 7th. It says:—

The troops shall debouch on your left in succession, as they come from the mountains. Push on—you will be successful. I expect the army within four or five days. As soon as your reply shall inform me of your march, I will set off to join you, probably by Pontremoli.

This is dated June 7th. Genoa is above 150 miles from Florence, and Macdonald broke up on the 9th. Can anything be more conclusive? He is to co-operate with an army, and to learn from Genoa where that army is; he is told all communication with it is cut off, and the confidential officer of its commander, recommends him to wait; he receives directions to march, and can hardly have read the letter, when he is off.

Jomini states that the Directory complained that:—

> He might have arrived towards the end of May, in the plains of Placentia; then, as Bellegarde was only descending from the Valteline, his junction with Moreau could not have failed between Tortona and the Trebbia; (adding from himself), to appreciate these observations, it is necessary to have before one the private correspondence of the generals.

It would seem not; for even, if Macdonald could have been quicker, when Jomini himself has told us that Moreau retreated towards Coni on the 17th May, and that his army was not extricated from the mountains before the 7th June, it can require no private correspondence to establish the querulous unfairness of the Directors' reasoning. It appears quite a fashion to traduce Macdonald. The author of the *Campagne des Austro-Russes* not only accuses him of causing the failure of the junction, but neglecting to consult the map, says, he (Macdonald) ought to have effected it by Sarzana and *Pontremoli!* He means, by the Corniche.

The following extracts from the correspondence already quoted, show who suggested (for, of course, Moreau only could command) the junction at Tortona.

Moreau's letter, 8th June, says:—

> I approve all your arrangements, &c.: from the obstacles the troops have met in passing the mountains, I shall confine myself to directing what I have nearest towards Bobbio, and shall debouch with the rest by the Bochetta and Novi. Nevertheless, if it be possible to move tomorrow evening, I will go by Pontremoli, but it is difficult.

His letter of the 11th says definitely, he shall be near Novi on the 16th or 17th. These difficulties, which, as we see, prevented the junction of the armies by Pontremoli, were consequent on Moreau's choice of a retreat from Alexandria by Asti on Coni, in preference to falling back on Genoa by Acqui and Savona, as Victor did. Had he done so, like that general, he could have reached Genoa on the 22nd May, and have joined Macdonald on the 30th.

Marshal Gouvion St. Cyr, who served in Italy in 1799, says on this much discussed question:

On the 29th May, Macdonald had his headquarters at Lucca—his right held the passes on Modena—his centre was at Pistoia, and Dombrowski, with the left wing, held Sarzana. Thus, the communication between the two armies was perfectly established, and one may say, their junction effected; but they would not have it so, because there were no good roads on which to pass artillery, as if they could not have embarked it at Lerici or elsewhere. They preferred hazardous operations.

The junction actually effected on the 29th May at Sarzana, was directed to be made in the middle of June at Tortona, where it was impossible it could be made; so that after the loss of much time and several battles, they were only too glad to come back a month later, to do what they should have done a month before. The Army of Naples, notwithstanding its losses at the Trebbia, found no difficulty whatever in thus effecting a junction with Moreau, which shows incontestably that those losses might have been avoided, and the union of the two armies duly effected at a much earlier period.

Both Macdonald and Moreau evidently saw more advantage in winning a battle near Parma than at the foot of the Bocchetta; but their best chance of winning anywhere depended on their union before the battle, and as Moreau did not choose to draw Macdonald to him, one wonders he did not defer his advance for the few days that were requisite to ensure their previous union.

CHAPTER 3

Fall of Alexandria and Mantua

A reinforcement of 11,000 Russians, under Rehbinder, more than replaced the casualties of the Trebbia. Kaim's force from Turin, and Haddick's from the Valais had joined Suwarow, who, early in June, could have marched 60,000 men against Moreau, while Macdonald would have been taken *in flagrante* in Tuscany. He expected the co-operation of the English fleet, and wrote to Nelson:—

> I trust the Baron of the Nile will soon be Duke of the Riviera di Ponente.

★★★★★★

Note:—At a somewhat later period, the following letters passed between Nelson and Suwarow:—

Dear Prince and Brother,

No man in Europe loves you as I do. All admire your brilliant achievements, as does Nelson, who more particularly respects you for your contempt of wealth. Duty makes you true and faithful to your monarch, and in this I dare to call myself your brother. I know my actions are not to be compared to yours; but the generosity of my sovereign rivals that of your own. The Emperor of all the Russias, the King of the Two Sicilies, and the Grand Signor, have overloaded me with honours and riches. In this respect we mutually present an example to the world of true service zealously rewarded. Today has made me the proudest man in Europe, for a certain person who has been near you for years, has told me that there are not two men living more alike in face, figure, and manners, than we are. We must be relations, and I beg you not to refuse me the dear title of your loving brother,

Nelson.

Prague,12th January 1800.

Dear Lord and Brother,

If any recollection will remain dear to me, it is that of resembling so distinguished an admiral as yourself. In looking at your portrait, I really do observe a resemblance between us, and thus it may he said, "*Lea beaux esprits se rencontrent.*" This new distinction enchants me; but even more than our likeness does our relationship rejoice me. There can be no rewards for your brilliant merits, dear admiral, in which your brother and friend does not take the warmest and most joyful interest. Jealous of this title and your friendship, I earnestly request you to continue your correspondence with me, and to be persuaded of the reciprocity of my feelings, which will always continue me your sincere friend and brother. Victory, glory, and good fortune for the new year.

Suwarow.

★★★★★★

But the emperor's autographic letters commanded him to attempt nothing until Mantua, Alexandria, and Tortona had fallen; declared that in no case would he tolerate any movements either into France or against Nice or Savoy; and as regarded the enemy's dislodgment from Liguria, he absolutely twice uses the precise expression of Sir Abel Handy when his checks on conflagration are none of them at hand—"perhaps it will go out of itself." On reading these effusions, Suwarow exclaimed,—"Thus are armies sacrificed," and immediately despatched additional men and artillery to Kray, and sent for a battering train to Alexandria, ordering Haddick to return to his former ground, which the Archduke Charles peremptorily refused to occupy, as he had been commanded.

If there be one of the strongly marked characteristics of Suwarow's practical and honest nature, which more than any other wins for him the cordial sympathy of all good men and true, it is the zealous manner in which in every instance he carries out the measures forced upon him by the Austrian Government, in direct breach of their promise to leave him independent, and in utter nullification of all his own plans of operation. In addition to this grievance, the council of war at Vienna was allowed to send orders to the individual generals employed in carrying out his orders, actually reversing them; while the Archduke Charles, when peremptorily ordered to relieve Haddick's corps on the St. Gothard, that it might join Suwarow's army to which it properly belonged, pertinaciously refused throughout the whole campaign to comply with these instructions.

Still we see Suwarow—provoked, and writhing under such contumacious injustice—in every instance earnestly exerting himself, and stimulating others, to carry out successfully the measures he disapproved, and cordially making the best of things as they were, in furtherance of the public good. But a few extracts from his letters will show the difficulty of his position far better than any general expressions. As early as the 27th May, he wrote from Turin to Rasumowsski, the Russian Ambassador at Vienna:—

Your Highness well knows that in the instructions I received on leaving Vienna, it is said with respect to Mantua that it shall be besieged or blockaded, as I think best. The latter was done, and Kray and Klenau, after effecting it, proceeded with the rest of their troops to join Ott, in order to obviate all danger to Mantua from the union of Montrichard and Gauthier with Macdonald. They were, however, suddenly recalled by the council of war, to besiege Mantua, without my having received the slightest intimation on the subject—so you see I am not wanted here. This decree disturbs the connection of all my operations, and in consequence I must prolong my stay at this place. I must send for Bellegarde. Haddick hesitates, and makes more danger for us. He comes to us weak, so that we are weak.

Each individual general addresses himself, not only on his own affairs, but on the general operations, to the council of war, and can thus intrigue for his own particular ends, so that the council, having the right to order them, can always shackle me. I could do much here with the Piedmontese troops, and arm them and maintain them without any cost to Austria. I could garrison towns with the best of them, and, with the troops they would liberate, act freely in the field; but now, garrisons take half our men. Was not this the grand rule of the French in their rapid conquests? Is it not the specious phrase "*Liberté et égalité*" that has trod down religion and sovereign power! If the council of war had left me unshorn, its work for two campaigns would not have cost me as many months; but with its power of hyper-*generalissimo*-ising, a month of its campaign would find me work for all the summer.

On the very day following that on which he thus complains of the council of war, we find him directing Kray, in obedience to their orders, to press the siege of Mantua with all his energy and means; and acquainting him, as regards the latter, that he has ordered Hohenzollern to join him from Milan, which would raise his force to 32,000 men. On the 6th July, he writes again to Rasumowski:—

So, the siege did not win us Turin! It was luck, in the Roman emperor's opinion! The directing Thugut knows the scales; he is always ready—so are pretexts. 'Oh! you require troops What would you do if you were beaten?' His Excellency does not know that to profit by victory, you must have troops; and now they want to take from me my poor lamb Rehbinder; and the archduke, while he carves so charmingly for himself, refuses to give me what he is ordered. Anger flows with the Tidone and the Trebbia. What will become of me? I must turn Cincinnatus. My late victories have cost me 5,000 men, but the fine talkers have cost me more than 10,000.

The general good would demand the replacement of these, and not the additional withdrawal of Rehbinder. If he leave me, I must leave this. Does the cabinet understand that no siege can be carried on without a corps of observation? I cannot by any means dispense with Rehbinder, nor with the relief of Haddick by the archduke. If His Highness's roof is to be covered, mine must not be left open. I wish these gentlemen would fight the French, instead of warring on me and the general good. Vienna cannot have the same insight into what is doing here, as I have. Let us have no more of these counsellors of war: all must depend on my truth, and confidence in me.

Again he writes:—

I wish to be away from this. Everywhere these counsellors of war with their unalterable routine will cause disaster. Security! Rule-preachers!—these latter have cost my army thrice as much, and the detached corps still more, than our three last battles—at least 10,000 men; while the order to relieve Haddick remains unfulfilled by the archduke, because His Highness talks like a book. They speak of some of Korsakow's people coming here, but, in the meantime, they take from me the Germans, as well as Rehbinder. Why should not the conquered countries undertake their own local duties, under the protection of the army? I have arms enough to give them.

The emperor desires that when I want to fight a battle tomorrow, I should first address myself to Vienna; as if circumstances in war did not change in a moment! Fortune is bald behind, but wears long locks in front; if you don't seize her by them, she will soon have her back to you. I never knew I was following Hannibal's teaching, either at the Trebbia or the Tidone, nor at Turin, where an accident gave us everything; nor at Milan, the gates of which I fancied had been opened to us by what we did at Vaprio and Cassano! Is one campaign or ten to be preferred? or is it better to have Paris as a goal to be speedily reached, or to block up the way to it by impediments we make ourselves? My friend and benefactor, give me full powers, or give me freedom.

At this period he wrote to the Emperor Paul:—

As our many victories and conquests have necessarily weakened the army, and as I have lost all hope in the archduke, the arrival of Rehbinder's corps was most opportune. Having strengthened Kray before Mantua, I have ordered Rosenberg (who now commands Rehbinder's division) to cover the siege and the conquered parts of Lombardy. The meddling nervousness of the council of war; their dislike of me as a foreigner; the intrigues of individual generals, who address themselves direct to it, and receive from it orders interfering with my operations; together with the impossibility of carrying out instructions sent to me by persons a thousand *wersts* from the scene of action; all oblige me, most respectfully, to solicit Your Majesty to recall me, if things are to continue thus. My only wish is to lay my bones in my own country, and to pray to God for my emperor.

The citadel of Alexandria surrendering on the 22nd July, after twelve days open trenches—during the last seven of which, 42,000 projectiles had been thrown into it—and a few days after, the more important one of Mantua having yielded—its garrison to march out on the 30th; Suwarow writes to Melas on the 31st:—

Mantua having fallen, we must no longer delay operations against the Riviera. Your Excellency knows, as well as I do, what we should gain, could we move at once. Whatever will facilitate our operations must be had, and we must take the responsibility on our own shoulders. Kray will be here in a week. In twelve days, we may be on the Col di Tende, and all our preparations for this must be ready in ten. The quickest measures are the best: don't hear of excuses. The object is of first-rate importance, and its results will repay double whatever it may cost us, I conjure Your Excellency, by your devotion to your sovereign, and your well-proved zeal, to employ alike your authority and your energy, that all our preparations may be completed within ten days. Rapidity is everything at this moment; delay a crime: there can be no excuse for failure. Report fully all you have done, and whatever is not completed, stating the reasons of the latter.

Suwarow's plan of operation here alluded to was, that Kray, Klenau, and Rosenberg should conjointly operate against Genoa, while he, personally, led a corps on Nice; so as to induce the enemy to evacuate Liguria for the defence of their own frontier, or to destroy them by a combined attack upon their flank, and rear, along the narrow line of the Riviera. But the month of July had been sacrificed, as regarded field operations, to the sieges of Alexandria and Mantua; the French in Liguria had been reinforced by Macdonald's people and fresh troops from France, so as now to number more than 40,000 men; while a considerable force was collecting in the maritime Alps, under Championnet, to co-operate with them.

As Kray's army from Mantua was approaching Suwarow, he issued one of his exciting and threatening proclamations to the Genoese; and to facilitate the impending operations, ordered an attack on Serravalle, which surrendered on the 7th August. Klenau, strongly reinforced, had cleared Tuscany of the enemy, and pushed along the Corniche road, as far as Sestri, and 12,000 men around Cherasco observed Championnet's force; when, on the 11th, 12th, and 13th of August, the French Army, near 40,000 strong, descended the Bocchetta, and the valleys of the Orba and Bormida, under the command of Joubert. "We must give the boy a lesson," was Suwarow's comment on hearing this intelligence. Joubert had begged Moreau to remain with him, and even to share his command. His friend replied:—

> Neither you nor I can sanction that arrangement, but I will not say farewell to Italy, till I have had the pleasure of fighting by the side of my brave Joubert.

On the 14th, soon after noon, the right of the French Army, under St. Cyr, had driven the Russian posts from Novi, and the left had halted behind Pasturana; while Joubert and his generals proceeded to reconnoitre the Allied Army encamped on the plain before them, and covering the siege of the citadel of Tortona, with its centre near the village of Pozzolo Formigaro. The extent of the encampment, and the masses of troops which their glasses showed them, moving in the direction of Bosco and Rivalta, at once convinced Joubert, that, contrary to his hope and expectation, Kray's force from Mantua must have joined Suwarow; when his perplexity and indecision became such, that he could literally resolve on nothing, and night had set in before he could bring himself to determine whether he would fall back or fight.

★★★★★★

Note:—It is so much a fashion, especially among a large literary class, to undervalue the highest military qualities as commonplace endowments, that it may not be altogether uninteresting to show, from St. Cyr's account of Joubert, at this moment, how wretchedly inefficient and incompetent the most admirable executive, and personally heroic officers may show themselves when called on to exercise the higher duties of command. St. Cyr states, that on returning to Joubert, after witnessing Suwarow's reconnaissance, he found him on the heights with Moreau, Dessoles, Sachet, and Perignon, the latter most impatient to rejoin his corps to put it in position. But Joubert was totally undecided what he would do, and seemed to regret that he had left the mountains. St. Cyr here remarks, that Joubert had served the Italian campaigns with the greatest distinction, but that now he afforded an example of the difference between carrying out the orders of an able chief, and exercising responsible command. Then he was all decision, now he was utterly without it.

He had simply to decide whether he would attack Suwarow, or retire into the Apennines. The first was absolutely irrational; the second, attended with no single inconvenience. For some time, the enemy had been preparing to attack Liguria, had even intended to have done so on the 12th, but circumstances had delayed him, and now the arrival of the French on the plain was a positive god-send to him. These considerations were urged on Joubert. There was no necessity to fight. Tortona would hold out, and use up the enemy's means, as long as its provisions lasted; in ten days Championnet might be in the plains with 35,000 men to co-operate. Should the enemy attack them in the mountains, the French knew every foot of the ground, and no affair of a few hours would there decide matters; but twenty actions sustained according to circumstances, on difficult ground, where the enemy's superior cavalry and artillery would be next to useless.

Joubert was assured that whatever he decided on should be zeal-

GENERAL BARTHÉLEMY CATHERINE JOUBERT

GENERAL JEAN VICTOR MARIE MOREAU

ously carried out, but he was entreated to decide at once, whether the army should retire or fight, and in the latter case whether the battle should be offensive or defensive; as in either, there was not a moment to lose in making the necessary dispositions: but Perignon and St. Cyr found it impossible to persuade their chief to decide on anything, and they went on talking until evening without the slightest result. From the windows of the casino where they sat, they could see all the enemy's dispositions, movements, and preparations for the battle. Perignon was on thorns to get back to his men, and to take up his ground. St. Cyr fortunately had occupied his: but he, too, was most anxious to be authorised to call in Watrin's division, which had been carried considerably too far to the right. Joubert, however, would not part with them till he had made up his mind.

At last he stated that he believed the best they could do would be to regain their former position, but that he feared they were too far advanced, and too near the enemy, to venture on a retrograde movement. St. Cyr combated this objection, urging that the night would conceal the movement, and that he, with the right, would check the enemy near Gavi, while the left fell back upon Savona.

This proposal, however, did not allay Joubert's indecision; which so agitated him, that he seemed ashamed of it, and begged the officers to excuse him: saying he had never before yielded to such weakness, that he had often been useful to Bonaparte, by offering suggestions in very difficult emergencies, and that he could not account for the irresolution, from which, at this moment, he found it impossible to free himself Finally, he seemed to have determined on a retreat, and told the generals to join their troops, and that in an hour or two they should have the orders to move; but they had seen too much of his fatal indecision to expect him to adhere to this opinion, and made what arrangements they could, rather for defence than retreat.

Perignon's people were asleep, and he contented himself with supporting the *védettes* they had thrown out, by a brigade. At nine o'clock St. Cyr again waited on Joubert, and found him as undecided as before, and on quitting him, was again told he had definitively determined on retreat, the orders for which should shortly be circulated—none, however, came, except a caution to keep the bivouac fires as much concealed as possible. At ten, Joubert sent word to St, Cyr, that from noises in the enemy's camp, it seemed they were retreating; to which St. Cyr answered they were drawing back their artillery into camp, and that he was persuaded they would attack the French at daybreak.

Thus, then, at midnight, of four French divisions, one only was in position—two were to take up their ground at daybreak, and the fourth was two leagues away, while within cannon shot lay a superior enemy, headed by a chief of desperate resolution; and yet, looking at these circumstances, from noon till midnight, a soldier, like Joubert, for want of one only of the thousand qualifications required to perfect a leader of armies, had continued paralysed to an absolute nullity.

Be assured, gentle reader, that a great commander is not a commonplace individual, and that Capt. Buck can scarcely be said to overstep hyperbole when he liberally admits that "Hannibal was a pretty fellow in his day."

Sir Walter Scott was somewhat of Capt. Buck's opinion. Mr. Lockhart says:

> I need hardly repeat that Scott never considered any amount
> of literary distinction as entitled to be spoken of in the same
> breath with mastery in the higher departments of practical
> life—least of all with the glory of a first-rate captain. Literary
> fame, he said, was a bright feather in the cap, but not the substantial cover of a well-protected head.

★★★★★★

While Joubert was still upon the Novi plateau, a couple of battalions were seen to quit the allied camp; and, advancing, to extend and lie down in the grain opposite the French *védettes*; while, from a group of staff officers behind them, a short figure, with nothing on but a shirt and trousers, rode forward, followed by a single orderly, and approached the French position. This was Suwarow, who, after making his observations, and occasioning a slight interchange of fire between the skirmishers, rejoined his staff. He naturally wanted his enemy on the plain; but, justly distrustful of his intention to advance, he had determined to attack, and would immediately have done so on this day, before the enemy's army was united, but that Kray's people required rest.

The Austrian generals are said to have been unanimous in opposition to Suwarow on this occasion, but he vehemently urged the danger of delay in a possible junction between Joubert and Championnet; made light of the strength of the Novi position and the quality of the enemy's troops; boasted of the gallant men he led, all accustomed to carnage and victory, and finally overruled them,—Melas characteristically remarking, that at the worst their numerous cavalry, which would

83

THE BATTLE OF NOVI

be next to useless in the battle, would effectually cover their retreat across the plain to Pozzolo.

The moment battle was resolved on, Kray solicited that to him and his countrymen might be assigned the honour of the grand attack, and Suwarow replied:—

> I assent to Your Excellency's proposition to attack the enemy at daybreak on the 15th, with all your forces, and I fully depend on you to dispose of his left wing. Attack him with the greatest impetuosity and drive him past Novi on Serravalle, *i.e.*, from the plain of the Lemme to that of the Scrivia, turning him as early as possible from Gavi. I will follow your attack in the plain with the troops from Pozzolo. I confide implicitly in my hero-friend!

To the troops he announced:—

> God wills—the *Czar* commands, and Suwarow orders that to-morrow the enemy shall be vanquished.

And the order for battle was simply:—

> At daybreak the corps of Generals Kray and Bellegarde (thirty battalions and twenty squadrons) will attack the left wing of the enemy at Pasturana, while the Russians (two divisions and reserve of cavalry) attack the centre, and Melas (thirteen battalions and sixteen squadrons) the right.

But most unaccountably the Russians were directed to advance at nine o'clock, and Melas at noon. The army amounted to full 42,000 men—6,000 were posted at Spinatti, and 13,000 remained around Tortona.

It would be difficult to conceive more favourable fighting ground for a brave army than that taken up by the French on the morning of the 15th August, on the plateau behind Novi. Its command of 100 feet or more over the plain in its front, and to the right and left along its whole extent of about a league, is perfect—it is only assailable from below by a stiff unbroken slope, breathing to mount, but good to charge down, and along which the fire of musquetry would sweep as over the glacis of a fortress; while in front of its right, the small town of Novi, compact within its walls and towers, protrudes like an immense bastion, giving a splendid flank command to right and left on anything assaulting the front of the plateau.

Its rear is effectually covered by a deep and rugged ravine, opening to the plain behind Pasturana, which separates and isolates the position from the neighbouring heights; except immediately in rear of Novi, where a narrow isthmus of its table ground trends backward, ascending gradually to the Monte Rotondo, and carrying with it the road to Gavi: the eastern falls of this ridge overlook the Serravalle road, which runs at their base, as well as the whole of the low ground intervening between it and the Scrivia.

These heights, the town of Novi and the ground behind it, were held, on the morning of the 15th August, by one of St. Cyr's divisions (La Boissière's) till the other (Watrin's) should arrive from Betoli di Novi by a circuitous route, the hostile fort of Serravalle being on the direct road. Grouchy and Lemoine's divisions, under Perignon, were to occupy the rest of the position to St. Cyr's left, with their immediate reserves in front of Pasturana. Dombrowski, who, with 3,000 men, blockaded Serravalle, was, if necessary, to support St. Cyr. Several country seats, half a mile or so apart, near the edge of the plateau, served admirably as points for observation, and the terraced grounds about them for the service of artillery.

At one of these, called Collinetta, not far to the left of Novi, so powerful a battery was established, as, with the flank defence of the town, to render an attack on that part of the position next to hopeless. On looking from this casino over the battleground, a soldier will almost sympathize with the fatal disinclination of poor Joubert to abandon it; but its fighting advantages are not a whit more evident to the meanest capacity, than is its grand defect in case of disaster. The deep and precipitous ravine which runs along its rear, restricts all retreat from it to the narrow isthmus along which goes the road to Gavi, on the extremity of the right flank, and the steep, zigzag defile of car-road which descends from Pasturana, on that of the left: the one an indifferent, the other a desperate communication for a retreating army; and both, from their position, lending themselves to almost certain seizure by an energetic enemy.

At daybreak on the 15th August, a dropping fire began on the left of the French advanced posts, and their troops rapidly stood to their arms. Joubert, the brave Joubert, galloped towards the left exclaiming as he passed, "Comrades, the republic orders you to battle," when shouts of "*Vive la république*," taken up from corps to corps, pealed lustily from end to end of the plateau, and welcomed the coming fight. The left wing of the army was hurriedly taking up its ground, when Joubert, riding in among the *tirailleurs* to keep them to their work in face of Kray's numerous columns, now pressing on to the attack, was shot dead. He was only in his thirtieth year! A private soldier in 1791, General of Brigade in 1796, he died in 1799.

But a short time before, he had married Madlle. de Montholon, sister of Lieut.-General the Count de Montholon, who accompanied Napoleon to St. Helena, and so faithfully served him to the last. He wore her portrait, and as he looked on it for the last time, he said, "I'll conquer: I have promised the republic, and I have promised her that I will do it, or die." He was cheering on his men below the villa called the Belyidere, waving his sword and crying, *"En avant, en avant! marchez toujours!"* and they were rallying at his words when he dropped lifeless from his horse.

★★★★★★

Note:—St. Cyr seems to imply that he sought his death, observing, that when he saw the enemy's columns advancing:—*"Il réaliza aussitôt ce que quelques mots qui lui, étaient echappés la veille, devaient faire prévoir. Il dit aux aides-de-camp dont il était entouré, 'jetons nous parmi les tirailleurs'—ce qu'ils firent au même instant. Il fut aussitôt atteint d'une balle qui le renversa mort."*

★★★★★★

On the death of their leader, the French light troops fled, and the Austrian columns, pressing up the slope in despite of the confused resistance of the forming troops, were already on the plateau, when Moreau by his exertions restored order; sent to St. Cyr for Colli's brigade, and, after a gallant and protracted struggle, succeeded in driving back the Austrians.

Kray, however, immediately re-formed his men on the plain below, and soon led them on, under cover of a furious cannonade, to a second attack; while Bellegarde led his cavalry round to the opening of the great ravine, to turn the left of the position. He had penetrated up a gully which opens on the plateau to the left of Pasturana, and the French front seemed yielding before Kray, when Perignon directed his reserve, in column of battalions, on the flank of Bellegarde's cavalry, while Richepanse, with his horsemen, charged their front. This vigorous movement cleared the flank of the position, and Kray was again repulsed by the superior numbers the enemy were now able to oppose to him.

On this second repulse (at near eight o'clock), Kray sent to press the attack of Bagration, who was waiting near Pezzolo in full view of the

French Army, for nine o'clock; but seeing Kray's difficulties he marched at once on Novi; before reaching which, he found himself checked by a battalion of light troops, with which Gardanne had most judiciously occupied the dry water channels in front of the town. Weak as was this force, notwithstanding the support received from Novi, yet by the most determined courage, the struggle against its numerous and brave assailants was so much prolonged, that St. Cyr particularises the fighting here as amongst the very hardest of the day; declaring that the ground had to be taken and retaken several times, before these admirable fellows were finally driven into Novi, against which Bagration's attacks were then directed, but utterly without success, and at a very serious cost; the height of the walls and the strength of the barricaded gates effectually baffling all attempts to escalade or storm them.

Repulsed in front, Bagration next attacked the French, left of the town; but this so fatally exposed his people to the artillery on the heights, that he soon abandoned it; and, re-forming his columns under the fire of the enemy's guns, desperately led them to assault the heights themselves. The perfect order and remarkable daring of this attack are highly eulogized by the French, who received it with a tremendous fire of round and grape; through which the Russians had already reached the slope of the plateau, and were pushing up, regardless of additional volleys of musquetry that now assailed them; when Gardanne's people, sallying from Novi on their left flank and rear, opened their fire at a stone's throw distance, and caused hesitation, then a halt, and finally irremediable disorder in their columns, which bodily fell back, and re-formed at some distance on the plain, under cover of their cavalry.

Suwarow was now entering the field at the head of Derfelden's men, when someone rode up, exclaiming, "the Russians are beaten."

"Are they all dead?" asked Suwarow.

"Not all," replied the speaker.

"Then they are not yet beaten," rejoined the marshal.

All were ordered to attack again, both to the right and left of Novi; Melas to march on the extreme French right and its rear, and troops from Spinetti and Tortona to hurry up as a reserve. Kray was, ere long, once more upon the enemy's position in front and flank; but, after all his efforts, was again repulsed. He, however, fell back fighting, and cut to pieces two battalions that pursued him, capturing General Partonneau, who led them on.

For two hours the Russians continued to reiterate their attacks on

Novi and the central heights, from which incessant showers of grape and musquetry plunged into their columns. Those attacking to the French right of Novi, were assailed by a sally from the town on their right flank, as well as by sustained attacks upon their left from Watrin's division, as its brigades successively took part in the battle, on their arrival from Betoli; and, after a strenuous resistance, they were eventually forced to give way. Their comrades on the other side of Novi, under Suwarow's more immediate observation, stood, or moved onward, in abortive attacks below the Collinetta, where Moreau and his strongest batteries were posted; suffering dreadfully under the concentric fire which poured from the natural rampart before them, and from the walls of Novi on their flank.

Whole regiments fell without a thought of flight; if others gave way, it was but to re-form to advance again: but all was unavailing. The carnage was dreadful; Suwarow frantically crying out, "Am I to be beaten at the end of my career?" tried to force his way to the head of the grenadiers, but his *aides-de-camp* seized his bridle (the staff having positive orders he should not unnecessarily expose himself), and the Allies fell back. The ardour of the French engaged them in a pursuit, which their generals vainly endeavoured to restrain, till the Russians turned fiercely upon them; when, apprehension for Moreau, whose horse was shot, induced them to halt and resume their ground upon the heights.

There was a lull along the line; the gathering of another storm. Orders were sent from the farm of San Marciano, where Suwarow had posted himself, to Melas, to take ground to his right, and attack Novi in front, while the Russians and Kray should again attempt the plateau; but Melas having already detached a column against Dombrowsky, and a brigade to turn the heights near Sarravalle, had but two brigades upon the field. With these he marched to the right rear of Novi. Watrin's troops, already wearied by their march and fighting, were recalled in haste from the plain to counteract this movement; and passing hurriedly over the difficult and broken ground that intervened, they arrived breathless and dispirited, to see Melas's columns at once advancing on their flank and rear.

They offered but a faint and most inadequate resistance to the Austrian brigades, which had gained the plateau with little loss; Calvin's Cisalpine troops, who occupied its slope, having, both officers and men, behaved disgracefully. St. Cyr finding it impossible to check the flight of Calvin's and Watrin's people, rode back to La Boissière's division behind Novi, and speaking a few words to the 106th demibrigade, led them headlong against the Austrian troops, now masters of the receding isthmus of table ground and the road to Gavi; and nobly did these gallant men fulfil the task before them, dashing like heroes through the superior Austrian force, and capturing General Lusignan and the two guns which were already sweeping the plateau.

This brilliant effort saved the French right wing from total destruction. Its fugitives escaped along the Gavi road—followed shortly by the troops from behind Novi; and before the astonished Austrians had recovered their self-possession, the glorious 106th, with their trophies—aided by the cavalry, where the ground admitted of its action—were seen slowly retiring and covering the rescued right wing, till it halted beyond the Riaffo and Tassarolo, scarce a league from the field of battle. Not so, however, with the left. While Melas was engaged as stated, the Russians were pressing hard on Novi, and Kray, in his tenth attack, was battling up the slope; the French, on the plateau, having to show front to north, east, and west, to cover their only line of retreat by Pasturana. Suwarow sent repeated orders to all the generals, and the purport of all and each was "forward, forward."

Melas and Bagration entered Novi on opposite sides nearly at the moment Kray's corps formed across the plateau. Shout after shout rose from the troops, as gradually the enemy was borne back on every side, stimulating higher and higher, at each succeeding burst, their furious zeal, and the rivalry of their comrades, till the fire of the allied musquetry had almost ceased, and the roar of cannon only broke above the loud hurrahs that marked their onward course. The French fought desperately to cover the passage of their guns through Pasturana, till an intelligent officer led some Hungarian light troops round to the rear of the village, and firing on the leading horses of the train, in a moment blocked up the road, when the confusion and slaughter became frightful.

★★★★★★

Note:—"I always add my hollo," said the yeoman, "when I see a good shot or a gallant blow;" and one cannot suppress a kindred feeling to that of the imaginary Locksley, in the idle pleasure of recording, however perishably, the names of junior officers who, with their limited means, have done good service. Major Kies commanded these Hungarians, and until his success produced the result it did, the loss of the French was trifling compared to that of the Allies. Dumas says, "*La bataille eut été presque sans ré-*

sultats si l'artillerie et les divisions qui formaient l'arrièrè garde eussent peu s'écouler par Pasturana;" and *"l'épouvantable boucherie"* are the terms used by other French writers to convey the effect of this (if even a soldier may be excused the epithet) happy movement.

★★★★★★

Lemoine's division was driven headlong down the great ravine by the Russians—Grouchy's was routed by the Austrians. One brigade only of the left wing (Grandjean's) had marched unbroken off the field. General Colli fought, while it was possible, in the streets of Novi, and then cut his way to Grouchy and Perignon at Pasturana. Here he fell mortally wounded, and Grouchy charging desperately, first with a standard in his hand, then with his helmet on his sabre—to encourage his men to make head against the enemy—sank under six, and Perignon under seven sabre wounds: all three falling into the hands of the enemy. Such was the devotion of these gallant men!

The battle was over at nine o'clock. Suwarow called it the fiercest and most obstinate he had seen, and "fury" and "enthusiasm" were the terms used in the despatches to describe the ardour of the troops. Upwards of 16,000 killed and wounded lay upon the plain and plateau, and 3,000 prisoners (including four generals), with thirty-nine guns, were the profits of this stubborn conflict. Suwarow's despatch terminates thus:—

I conclude with the solemn assurance, uttered by a heart brimful of joyful feelings, that from the general to the private of the Imperial Army, all have shown a bravery at which I wonder, but which I cannot describe. I thank God for having; commanded so glorious an army, and with deep gratitude to it, I unite my voice to the testimony which General Melas gives in favour of the noble men whose conduct he is able to particularise.

No pursuit was undertaken; though such was the condition of the French Army, that on the 17th (two days after the battle) Moreau wrote to St. Cyr that Colli had arrived at Campo Freddo, and that he trusted Perignon had resumed his original position—both these generals being at the time in the hands of the enemy, and the commander-in-chief knowing nothing of them, or of the dispersed remainder of their troops. Some idle firing, in which both sides claimed the advantage, took place on the 16th, between the French right and the Austrians, who had pushed back Dombrowsky; after which both armies and their respective outposts resumed the positions held by them before Joubert's advance.

There are few battles the perusal of which will not make the coldest critic something of a partisan; but Novi is not one of these, for it is doubtful in the impression it leaves, whether our sympathies are most deeply interested for the heroism that conquered, or for that which was vanquished. Novi did no credit to any quality of Suwarow's, but his indomitable perseverance. Adopting most fully his opinion of the necessity of fighting (for who would allow 40,000 men to strengthen a position like that of Novi, within a march of a place besieged, when another hostile army was daily expected to cooperate with it?), it is impossible to understand the motive of his decision, that Kray's attack should be carried on for four hours utterly without support.

Looking at the Novi position as one peculiarly lending itself on both sides to a flank attack, many might have considered, under the circumstances that existed, an operation against its right, with the *appui* of Serravalle on the outer flank of the attacking; army, to be a juster movement than that adopted by Suwarow; but it is, nevertheless, certain that the one sanctioned by him, as explained in Melas's report, *viz.*,—the attack by Kray, embracing the left wing of the enemy in flank and rear, to push it past (*i.e.* behind) Novi on Serravalle, turning it, as the ground rendered practicable, from Gavi, was an operation which, if duly supported by a timely co-operation by Bagration against the right of the enemy's left wing, must, as admitted by the enemy, have been attended with triumphant and profitable results.

Kray's operation, however, either from the original misdirection of his columns, or from the consequences of his repulse, soon assumed the character of an attack on the front, rather than the flank of the enemy's left wing; so that when Bagration came upon the field, the occupation of the ground by the Austrians obliged him to lead on Novi instead of well to the French left of it, and originated the bulldog like assaults on Novi and the formidable plateau on either side of it: in which, to use Suwarow's own words:—

His soldiers exhausted by heat and thirst, in face of a position by nature strong as a fortress, preferred destruction to retreat; and exhibiting a superhuman perseverance, in their blind and desperate courage, stormed through a hail of missiles, and disregarding every obstacle, rushed on inevitable death.

This frightful struggle, as he justly styles it, never would have taken place, had the troops been so disposed and directed as to support each other when necessary; and it was unquestionably the bounden duty of Suwarow, that, on ground overlooked on every inch of its whole extent by the enemy, the troops should have been so placed, and so instructed.

Suwarow had every advantage that circumstances can give to an attacking general: superior numbers; excellent troops; time to make his dispositions; and perfect knowledge of his enemy's ground. And yet he was saved apparently from an ignominious defeat solely by the almost miraculous success of two weak brigades, which showed such hesitation and irresolution in their advance, that it is said the merest appearance of vigour would have checked them; but before which—such is war!—three full brigades of French soldiers fled like a mob, scarce offering resistance.

We learn, however, from his unconquerable perseverance, what a determined will may do to palliate the consequences of a vicious combination; for though we dare not say it would of itself have conquered, we know it occupied the enemy so entirely as to enable Melas's weak force to carry out successfully his judicious and decisive movement. Never was a battle more strangely planned or more heroically fought than that of Novi!

★★★★★★

Note:—On coming down to breakfast at the "Black Eagle," we encountered our first memorial of the battle in the mark of a musket-shot under the cornice of the room, with the date inscribed below it—"*15th Agosto* 1799." The guide provided for us was a respectable-looking lame old soldier, who said he had served at Austerlitz and Eylau, and had been twice wounded, but who, though recommended to us as "*parfaitement instruit*," I soon found knew next to nothing of Novi; and it pained me to find in his conversation an obtrusive exhibition of shallow infidelity, so that when I set out for Pasturana, I was not sorry to avail myself of his lameness as an excuse for dispensing with his further services.

The road, from the Gavi gate of Novi to this village, diagonally crosses the French position. The day was glorious, and showed me all I came to see most famously. The walk is chiefly along the edge of the great ravine or valley which backs in the position, except immediately behind the town and castle of Novi. Pasturana is most picturesquely placed with its *castelletto* on the right of the steep road and defile which goes down to the Riasco, and a precipitous bank upon its left. It is very pretty, but a deadly thing to look at, as the only passage of a routed army.

When I drank to Major Kies in the Riasco water, I did not forget Grouchy and Perignon and Colli. I looked up, and thought of Lemoine's division. Good heavens!—could a bone in their bodies have come down unbroken? No wonder the Frenchmen write of *"l'épouvantable boucherie;"*—it could be no less with earnest men under furious excitement on such ground as this. How beautiful, peaceful, and sunshiny it all lay before me! I had walked up to a height, between the village and the next ravine, towards Bassaluzzo, where a religious mission had yesterday put up a gigantic crucifix, and as I was intently peopling the ground before me with Bellegarde's and Richepanse's battling horsemen, a man came suddenly round the bushes and disturbed me; it was a priest—one of the mission from Genoa. I bowed to him, and he to me.

A half-expended soldier and a youthful priest exchanging courtesies on a whilom battlefield, where all else was stillness, cheerful sunshine, dappled light and shadows, and a universal beauty that quite stirred the heart, formed a picture somewhat different from that I was endeavouring to conjure up. God grant that past and present may long continue to offer such contrasts! As I was singing my way back, I came bolt upon an old peasant, who stared for a moment, and then broke into a shout of *"Allegre, allegre!"*

Altogether, I think a day may be well passed at Novi.—*Extract from a Journal.*

★★★★★★

CHAPTER 4

Suwarow Ordered to Switzerland

After this victory, so completely did Genoa and the French Army appear at the mercy of Suwarow, that Moreau prepared to evacuate the city, and had even embarked his artillery, awaiting the farther orders of the Directory; while Klenau, reinforcing himself with all the troops and peasants he could collect from Tuscany, had advanced within a march of Genoa, in the hope of carrying it by surprise or force. But Klenau was repulsed, and Suwarow temporarily diverted from Moreau by the movement of Championnet and Lecourbe, who respectively threatened Piedmont from the maritime Alps and the St. Gothard; the latter having carried all the Archduke Charles's posts in the Reussthal and pushed back Haddik's advance with serious discomfiture. Forces were marched against them, and headquarters fixed centrically at Asti on the 20th August.

From this place Suwarow reiterated his desire to be recalled; and whoever peruses the puerile despatches which reached him in shoals, under the signature of the Emperor Francis, incessantly prescribing; measures which Suwarow's successes had thrown completely *hors de ligne*—ordering away generals and strong bodies of troops, and then apprizing Suwarow that he (the emperor) had done so, and positively forbidding the execution of the measures requisite to secure the Italian conquests—will readily sympathise with the indignant bitterness with which he declares:—

I can serve here no longer. The orders hourly arriving from the council of war make me ill. At a thousand *wersts* from the scene of action, they will direct operations, in total ignorance of what is going on. Here is a new order from the council. You will judge from it whether I can stay here any longer. Lay it before

His Majesty, and solicit my recall the moment the Genoese operations are over. I am weak and can write no more.

To Rostopchin he writes:—

> You will see from my despatch that the Austrian system for the protection of the gates of Vienna has upset everything here. I literally know nothing of what is doing. Everything is regulated by the council of war. I cannot tell you how exhausted I am. I am altogether a superfluous member of this army, and simply the executor of Dietrichstein's orders. I try to bear up against it like a man, but I must find a refuge from it, whether in a cottage or a coffin.

Tortona having capitulated on the 22nd (to surrender in twenty days if not relieved) and Lecourbe having retired up the St. Gothard, the army was once again assembled at Asti for the advance on Genoa, when Suwarow's further proceedings in Italy were abruptly put a stop to by an order he received from Vienna to march with his Russians to take the command in Switzerland. The Emperor Paul had entered on this war with the old-fashioned disinterestedness of a *Preux Chevalier*, to restore dethroned kings and desecrated religion; but the cabinet of Vienna preferred to consider the conquests of the French in Italy as "*faits accomplis*," which had annihilated all pre-existing claims.

Suwarow had been desired by Paul to invite the king of Sardinia to Turin, to replace him on his throne, and to maintain him there; and Suwarow's letter of the 4th August to the Emperor Francis, reporting the expected arrival of His Sardinian Majesty, was crossed *en route*, by one of the day previous from Francis to him, saying that he had persuaded Paul of the disadvantages attendant on the king's immediate return to Piedmont, and desiring Suwarow to arrest everything in progress for this measure till he should hear further. This was a state of things that could not last, and the Austrian cabinet terminated it by hurriedly carrying out an arrangement which had been some time in deliberation, and despatching the Russians and their leader to a country which offered more to overcome and less to discuss than the almost subjugated Italy.

★★★★★★

Note:—One of the most plausible of the several false and shallow pretexts set forth by the Austrian cabinet in favour of this measure, was the rivalry and jealousy said to exist between the Russian and Austrian

EMPEROR PAUL I

troops; but this, as regarded the Italian Army, was utterly groundless. Rivalry and emulation there were, as it was natural and beneficial there should be, but nowhere in Italy, from first to last, do we see one instance of such rivalry exhibiting itself to the detriment of the public service. Deprecating, as Suwarow did, a system like that of Austria, which paralyzed a commander by the interference of the council of war with his subordinates, he fully and cordially appreciated the individual merits of its officers.

Of Melas, he always speaks as a worthy, honourable, good, and gallant man. Of Kray the same; adding, "he would be the best successor to me you could find." Wuckassovich, Klenau, Kain, Alcaini, &c., he mentions as men he highly values. Of Chastelar and Zach, we read in his correspondence:—

My good-natured, giddy-pated weathercock—the brave Chastelar—has gone and got himself foolishly wounded at Alexandria, and they have sent me Zach—good, quiet, and learned, but a true project-smith and security man. God grant Chastelar his health!

Indeed, the only instance in which he expresses dissatisfaction with an Austrian officer is when he says of Bellegarde's gratuitous reverse at San Juliano:—

The wise Bellegarde is one of the system-mongers. At the outset of the war he favoured the enemy with 10,000 of his men, and today in my necessity he has played away 2,000 for me.

Of the Austrian troops he never writes but in the most cordial terms. "The Germans always do their duty, and fight well with me," he says, "why should it be otherwise elsewhere?" And with respect to any estrangement between them and his own people, he triumphantly scoffs at the bare idea of such a state of things; emphatically and justly declaring "there can be no disunion in the united army while I retain my senses. I laugh at the jabber of the system-mongers, who just hit the mean between your fool and rogue!" And when all was over on the 20th October, we find him writing: —

Throughout the late campaign in Italy it was impossible a better understanding could exist between our troops and the Allies. This was in the order of things, and as was natural. Zeal on both sides gave the hand to assist, and in all things made up for every deficiency.

★★★★★★

According to this new plan, Melas, with his Austrians, was to act in Italy; Suwarow with his countrymen, Condé's corps, some Bavarians and newly embodied Swiss, in Switzerland; supported on his right by a German Army styled the "Intermediate:" which, under the Duke of Wurtemberg, was to take post about Stockach or Donauschingen, and communicate with the Royal Imperial Army under the Archduke Charles on the Rhine; which again was to give its hand to the Duke of York, who, with a combined force of British and Russians, was expected speedily to liberate Holland and the Netherlands.

On the 28th August, Suwarow acknowledged the receipt of the order to march to Switzerland, declaring himself ready to move the moment Tortona should surrender; but at the same time he strongly urged on the emperor the propriety of not removing the Russians from Italy, until Coni should have been taken, and the enemy driven from Liguria, Nice, and Savoy; which he says might be effected in two months: and so strong did he consider the representation made by him on this subject, that in notifying to the archduke and Korsakow the order he had received, he tells them he has no expectation of being with them before the expiration of the period mentioned.

But he little knew the men he had to deal with. To his astonishment, on the very day after he had thus written, he learned that the archduke was preparing to leave Switzerland; when he thus addressed him:—

I have received the extraordinary news that Your Highness considers it your duty to leave the Russian troops alone in Switzerland, so speedily, that you have already commenced your march towards Suabia. The inevitably disastrous consequences of this measure for Germany and Italy, must be evident to so experienced a general as Your Highness. I am persuaded your zeal for the public good will prevent the precipitate execution of an order so detrimental to our objects, and so much increasing the difficulty of attaining them. Confident in your penetration and right intention, I cannot but feel at ease in this respect, and I feel sure of hearing the agreeable news of the fresh victories for which Switzerland will be indebted to Your Highness before you leave that country.

Long, however, before this letter reached the archduke, he had already marched, and on the 29th August, had reported to Suwarow, not only that he had done so, but that he had gone, utterly disregarding the positive orders of his government to recover the line of the St. Gothard, lost to the Allies by the defeat of his left wing on the 15th August; thus adding to Suwarow's difficulties by leaving the nearest line by which his march could be effected, in the hands of the enemy. This movement of the archduke necessarily precipitated measures, every consideration giving way to the urgent necessity of reinforcing the inadequate body now left exposed to attack in Switzerland.

Suwarow's prophetic comment on the prospect before him was thus briefly penned on the back of his instructions:—

1st. We want troops, clothing, and supplies of every kind. 2nd. We shall have to fight often on difficult bad ground, lose men, and be weak when we arrive. 3rd. Masséna need not wait for us to beat us; let him throw himself on Korsakow who is close to him, then on Condé, and that will do.

But Suwarow's energy seemed more excited by the additional difficulties thus heaped upon him; and believing, as he did, on the 3rd September, that only 11,000 of his troops would accompany him into Switzerland (Rehbinder's division being then under orders for Malta), he reported himself prepared to move, the moment Tortona's surrender should leave him free to do so.

At the end of August, after the archduke and his army of 35,000 men had marched for Germany, the Limmat, the Linth, and the lakes of Zurich and Wallenstadt, separated the French and the Allies in Switzerland. Korsakow with 25,000 Russians held Zurich and both banks of the Limmat, opposed to Masséna and 37,000 French, upon Mount Albis. Hotze, with 22,000 Austrians or Swiss occupied the long line from Rapperschwyl, on the lake of Zurich by Wesen and Wallenstadt, to Dissentis in the Rheinthal, (*thal*, signifying valley, when joined to the name of a river, designates the valley through which such river runs), and was opposed to Soult, who had an equal number of men partly massed on the left of the Linth, and the remainder occupying the valley of the Reuss and the St. Gothard.

On the 5th September, Suwarow informed the Allied generals in Switzerland that he purposed joining them by the St. Gothard, and after effecting their junction, marching by the shores of the Lucerne lake, to co-operate in a general attack on the enemy, so as to unite their victorious forces on the lower Reuss and Aar. He called their attention to the left, saying:

I expect, before all else, the co-operation and junction of

100

Linken with me in the way he thinks best, as on this junction all subsequent success depends.

Recommending, if necessary, this officer's strong reinforcement, and requiring information from him and Hotze as to the spot where they could most speedily and safely connect their forces; concluding by requesting that the troops might be daily exercised in attacks by column with the sabre and bayonet.

On the 8th, he took leave of the Austrian Army of Italy. He said:

No words can express the satisfaction I have experienced in commanding so brave and well-disciplined an army, nor the grief I feel at parting from. it. The impression made on me by the steady intrepidity of the Austrians cannot be effaced. Let them be assured I shall never forget the love—the blind confidence they showed me; to which I owe the palm of victory.

Further movements of Moreau and Championnet caused his troops, which had already marched, to return to Alexandria; but after a solemn religious ceremony, and distribution of honours to the officers and soldiery, he, himself, receiving the *Czar's* portrait and the title of Prince Italisky, on the 11th of Sept. (the citadel of Tortona surrendering on that day) the effective remnant of near 40,000 marched on Taverne, which was headquarters on the 15th.

Here, contrary to the assurances he had received, neither mules nor provisions had arrived, and having made forced marches to this point, he had to remain till the 21st. In explaining his position to Paul, he says:—

Lord Mulgrave assures me that the English ministry had no idea of your Imperial forces entering Switzerland until the archduke should have freed it from the enemy, and that Thugut had solemnly assured them that the archduke would not leave Switzerland, and that he would write again to His Highness; but, in the meantime, while they write, the prince is allowed to effect his movement. On leaving the army on the 11th, I demanded from Melas the full number of mules required for my march; but he only gave me those required for the mountain guns, declaring all the others would be ready at Bellinzona. By forced marches we came to Taverne (ten *versts* from Bellinzona), and find no single mule arrived; and here have we been five days idle. This inactivity is a great advantage to the enemy, who can adopt measures that may seriously endanger us. In this desperate position I saw nothing for it but to dismount our Cossacks and use their horses instead of mules—an expedient which, to our great consolation, was suggested by Prince Constantine. Four hundred mules have since arrived, and with these we shall commence our march.

General Melas subsequently stated in his explanation, dated Savigliano 22nd, that 1,344 mules had been despatched by Pavia, to arrive at Bellinzona on the 11th, but that the Austrian commissary, Ruprecht, had stopped them at Pavia to load them with oats; and as an additional illustration of the strange way of doing business in this department of the Austrian Army, the mules, which eventually arrived, 650 in all, were only hired to go to Bellinzona, where a fresh agreement had to be made with their *capitani*. Finally, however, these and the Cossack horses being laden with ammunition and provisions for six days (the soldiers each carrying four days bread), and the field guns (except the mountain two-pounders) sent round by the Splugen, the Russians were enabled to resume their march, for the conduct of which the following instructions were issued:—

The mountain paths are in general so narrow that an unloaded horse can scarcely turn on them—much less a laden mule. The columns must be so formed as to obviate this difficulty. The guns and what belongs to them must never be either at the head or the rear of columns, as in the one case they would impede the march, and in the other not be easily got at when wanted. Our object being to do all possible damage to the enemy, nothing can be worse for us than anything leading to hesitation or falling back. Each of the two infantry divisions will form a separate column, unless the whole army move upon a single path. The division column is to be thus formed: where the ground allows them to act, twenty-five Cossacks, then twenty armed pioneers, followed by a battalion of *jägers* or grenadiers, with one gun and its appurtenances. Then three battalions and a gun—two battalions and a gun—and four battalions with two guns, similarly apportioned, followed by ten mules, with spare flints and ammunition.

After the divisions, the Cossack horses and mules with provisions, followed by the baggage, under the protection of a battalion and 100 Cossacks. When the guides say we are approaching a defile, the leading Cossacks will fall back and *jägers* be pushed on; the divisions to close up with intervals of 200 paces between them. To take a hill occupied by the enemy, a detachment proportioned to its extent, must extend and ascend it—the remainder following at 100 paces distance. At turns in the mountain where the enemy's fire does not tell, the men will take breath, and then go on afresh. Should the light troops be checked by the obstinate resistance of the enemy, and not be able to get on, the column must then, without firing, and with the greatest impetuosity, dash forward on the hill and attack it with the bayonet.

If the enemy is at all shaken, he will not wait for this attack, but easily give way. No hill can be carried by firing only, as scarcely any damage can be done to the enemy on it; the shot either not reaching, or going over him, while his fire from above is far more effective—so that the utmost exertions must be persevered in, to gain the summit of the hills as rapidly as possible, that we may not remain exposed to fire. No hill need ever be attacked in front, if its flank can be got at. Whenever the enemy shall have neglected to occupy the highest points of ground, these must be seized as soon as possible, and be attacked from above with fire and bayonet.

In the more particular disposition for the attack on the St. Gothard and Reussthal, we read:—

In the attack on the enemy's right, we come on a force of 20,000 men, to which we can oppose more than 35,000.

Which clearly shows the extent of Austrian co-operation on which he calculated, his own force barely amounting to 20,000: and his final letter to Korsakow and Hotze from Bellinzona, on the 23rd, says:—

You will see from the enclosed plan and disposition how I mean to cross the St. Gothard, and to attack in the Reussthal. You will co-operate simultaneously with me, freeing the small cantons and overcoming our first obstacles. But how and when? All this must be left to your own arrangement for best meeting the local difficulties and the opposition of the enemy. All I can say to you is, that no difficulty is to be considered insuperable—no opposition too formidable—but that everything must be done, even at extraordinary sacrifices, to effect the grand result at which we conjointly aim. We must shrink from nothing, and we may be sure that, with determination and active energy, all we have to do will be done. Every delay strengthens the enemy and adds to obstacles which the mere difficulties of movement and provisioning the troops hourly make more formidable. I trust, therefore, that every corps will punctually do whatever is prescribed for it, at the time laid down. For all our sufferings and hardships, the blessings of the liberated countries, the favour of our illustrious monarch, and the praises of the world, will amply reward us.

On the small plateau of the St. Gothard, seven thousand feet above the sea, are several small lakes, two of which are the sources of the Ticino and the Reuss. The road from Bellinzona to Altorf ascends the valleys and chasms by which the former of these streams rushes down from the mountain, and descends those by which the Reuss pours downwards on the northern side; but in 1799, this was a mere mule road, of which the traveller still recognises frequent remains, especially near the summit of the pass. Ten thousand French, under Lecourbe—a name immortalised in mountain warfare—occupied this line, which offers many points where a few brave men might check an army.

In the two leagues from Airolo to the summit, it ascends 3,000 feet, crossing the Ticino at the Ponte Tremolo; above which the long defile, scarce broad enough for the narrow road, is closed in by sheets of rock, till it opens on an amphitheatre of rugged and precipitous ground, lending itself to a deadly concentric fire upon its narrow issue; and in the steep descent of eight leagues to Amsteg, down the Krachenthal or Crashing valley, the roadway is in many places cut into the walls of rock, below which roar and rush along the cataract and torrent of the Reuss. Across these the road passes several times—at the Devil's Bridge by an arch of 70 feet span, and at the Monk's Leap by one of 90. Such obstacles, and so defended, might be deemed insurmountable to direct attack; but they may be turned by paths crossing the mountains, which rise with their glaciers between the Rhine and the Reuss, ascending the lateral valleys that supply torrents to the former river, and descending with those which contribute to the latter.

For this purpose. General Rosenberg, with 6,000 men, had marched from Taverne by Bellinzona and the Val di Blegno, on the 19th, to pass the Lukmainier and Oberalp, and descend to the Urserenthal, turning the St. Gothard; while General Auffenberg, with four battalions, was

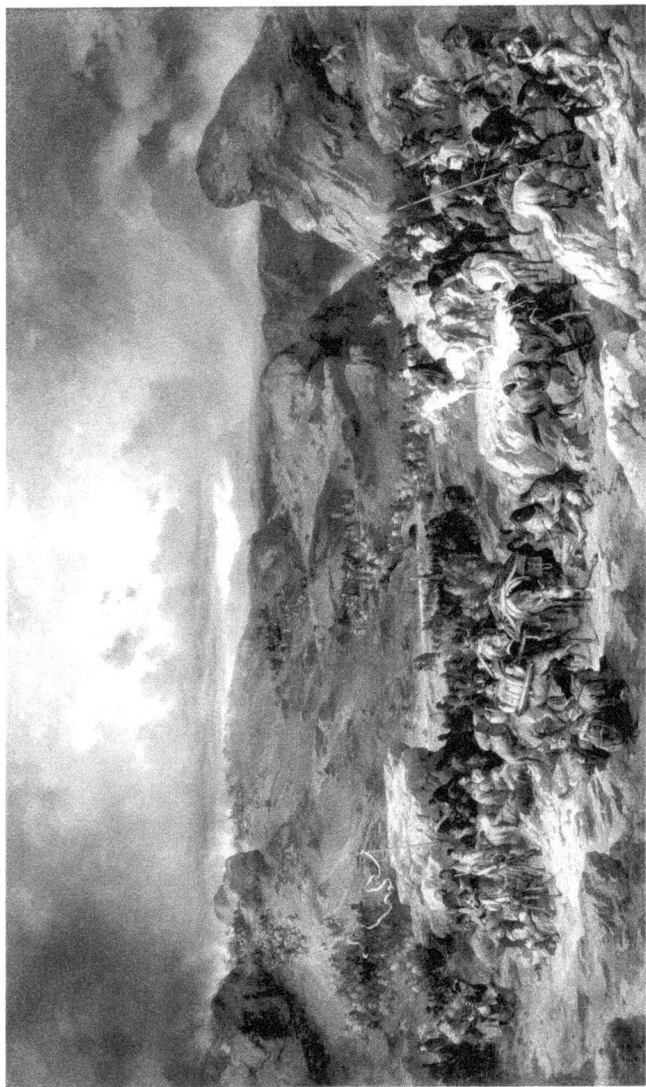

St. Gothard taken by Suwarow's troops in 1799

to leave the Rheinthal at Dissentis, to cross Mount Crispalt by the hunter's path, and come down on Amsteg by the Maderanerthal, in rear of the Monk's Leap bridge and other obstacles. Generals Linken and Jellachich were expected to unite 9,000 men of Hotze's force in the Glaris valley, to pass Mount Bräghel, and, entering the Muottathal, to effectuate their junction with Suwarow towards Schwytz; while Hotze himself, occupying Einsiedeln, should connect his operations with theirs by the Haken Pass, or Rothenthurm, and with Korsakof's from the Zurich side; all to be prepared for a general attack upon the enemy, with their combined forces, on the 26th September.

Suwarow, leaving Taverne on the 21st, made successive marches to Bellinzona, Giornico and Faido; and on the morning of the 24th, approached Airolo, at the foot of the St. Gothard, where Gudin, with three or four French battalions, was ready to receive him. His main body moved direct on Airolo by the mule road, while Colonel Strauch, with a detachment, threatened the enemy's right flank; and Schwei-kowsky's division, with Bagration's advance guard, leaving Faido at three in the morning, had divided their force, after passing at some distance the enemy's left; one portion remaining to turn Airolo and its immediate defences, and the remainder proceeding by a long and most difficult detour to scale the glaciered mountains, and descending from them on the plateau of St. Gothard, to take all the other obstacles of the ascent in reverse.

It is reported that when the Russian main column reached the Stalvedro defile, where the mighty St. Gothard is first fully seen towering with its eternal snows into the clouds, it simultaneously halted and ordered arms, while a complaining murmur passed from man to man. At the words, "Come, boys, march on—the enemy's close by at Airolo," they shouldered and marched on, and shortly after encountering Gudin's advance, pushed forward with a steady courage; which, seconded by the flank attacks of Strauch's and Bagration's people, soon won them Airolo. Above the village, however, their progress was much slower. The enemy from the higher ground availed themselves of all its advantages, and often swept the successive ascents they had to win with a fire that told fatally upon them; they were raw and untrained at this kind of fighting, while their enemies were masters in its art; on many spots it was impossible to act with the bayonet; three of their commanding officers were successively shot down; perhaps the impression of the St. Gothard had damped their morale: at all events in one part of the ascent the whole attacking line fell back.

Suwarow was furious—he threw himself from his horse into a ditch, and called on them to bury him on the spot where his children had disgraced themselves. "I am no longer their father!" he exclaimed. They rallied—returned under the fire, and, impelled by rage and shame, desperately won their way inch by inch up the grand and steep Val Tremola to its formidable *debouché* on the plateau; where vainly striving to climb where unencumbered men could scarcely hold their footing, they were exposed to the terrible concentric fire of the enemy, whom the ground effectually covered; till the appearance of Schweikowsky's men descending to the plateau from the higher peaks and ridges, led to the enemy's immediate and hasty retreat.

Shouting with delight, the infuriated Russians raced after them with fire and bayonet over the plateau, and down the whole descent to the village of Hospital in the Urseren valley; where the French turned towards Realp and the Furca, and the Russians, as dark night had now set in, established their bivouac. On the plateau of the St. Gothard, just where the steep descent on the Italian side begins, the words "Suvarof Victor," rudely cut in a mass of rock near a zigzag of the old road, still form a simple but eloquent appeal to those who there look down upon the most formidable scene of this day's noble struggle. But with the earnest and heroic men here met in arms, the close of day in no degree ensured the close of battle; and as Suwarow rode down in the night to join his men at Hospital, loud and sustained firing reached his ears, both from the direction of his front and to his right.

His gallant enemy Lecourbe, having left detachments on the Oberalp and at the Devil's-Bridge, had posted himself with 6,000 men in the Urseren valley between Hospital and Andermatt; having his reserve at the latter village, whence it could support his force, or that on the Oberalp, as required. Night had scarcely set in, when, almost simultaneously, he saw in his front the rapid play of fire down the road from the St. Gothard, from Suwarow's and Gudin's men, followed by heavy discharges first above and then through Andermatt, and onward in his rear towards the Umerloch and Devil's-Bridge.

The latter came from Rosenberg's force; which, after a succession of actions during the day, in front of and along the Oberalp lake, had pushed the party opposed to them near to Andermatt, and then apparently held back for an hour or more till they should see signs of Suwarow's people approaching Hospital, which the ground they held enabled them to do. The moment their flashes appeared, they fell on so vigorously that, routing their immediate antagonist, and Lecourbe's reserve alike, they carried all before them in *pèle mèle* confusion to the Devil's-Bridge; which, after such resistance as enabled the mass of fugitives to escape, was hurriedly blown up.

Lecourbe's position thus seemed desperate. Shut in between the mountain and glacier of St. Anna on the one side, and on the other the rapid Reuss, with not even space between them to deploy his men— the bridge over which lay the only road of his retreat destroyed—and 6,000 enemies not two miles away between it and him in rear; while Suwarow, with 12,000 in his front at Hospital, not half a mile distant, barred him from the Furca path; he had nothing in his favour but the darkness, and his own glorious decision: and—true soldier that he was!—he required no more. His troops were ordered rapidly to ford the Reuss, while the whole of his artillery opened a sustained fire on the Russians, closely bivouacked about Hospital; and when his men were over, he without a moment's hesitation, threw all his guns into the stream, and with his whole force mounted the vast ridge of rock that rises between the valleys of Urseren and Goschenen, and, descending to the latter in the morning, reached the road behind the Devil's-Bridge, and proceeded by it towards Wasen. Early on the 25th, Suwarow joined Rosenberg at Andermatt; where, though some provisions were captured, want was already so severely felt that it is said the men greedily devoured all the soap and hides they could discover.

As soon as the troops were formed, the attack on the Devil's-Bridge began. Just above and close beside the excavated tunnel of the Urnerloch, the Reuss drops as it were out of the Urseren valley, and dashes downward in a magnificent fall of three hundred feet, through a chasm of the rocks which rise like walls on either side of the thundering torrent, across which the bridge affords the only passage. Its arch being sprung, as already stated, and the rock on the French side forming a perfect wall, from which fire and stones could be showered on every inch of the ground between the Urnerloch and fall, nothing could be hoped for from a direct attack. In fact, till the bridge should be restored it was simply impossible for any human being to cross the torrent at this point.

A detachment of two hundred volunteers, under Major Trewogün, had consequently been ordered to ford the Reuss near Andermatt, and to scale the rocks so as to descend from above on the defenders; but their progress was too slow for Suwarow's impatience at this moment, when so much depended on his timely junction with his allies, and his noble soldiers were allowed to debouche from the Urnerloch,

The battle at Devil's-Bridge

and to dash down upon the broken bridge and yawning chasm. Their leading files were naturally swept away at once by the enemy's fire; but the column pressing forward, the steep slope between the cavern and the bridge soon became, and long continued, crowded with men, who rapidly sank down or disappeared, and were renewed as they fell under the fire that poured on them, or were forced into the abyss beneath.

In vain was the word passed that the passage was impracticable; the voices were lost amid the musquetry and the roar of the cataract, and great numbers of first-rate soldiers perished there miserably, before order could be restored. At length the mass was drawn back, and a steady fire was opened across the chasm, from the rocks by the Urnerloch and to its right, so as to occupy the enemy until the descent of the flanking party from the crags above on their rear and right flank obliged them to retire precipitately.

Beams and planks were immediately run across the broken arch, lashed together with cords and sashes, and over this frail path (from which some, confused by the whirl of water, or blinded by the spray swept up in violent gusts, fell into the Reuss), the advance passed rapidly, and pushed on by Wasen as far as the Monks Leap-bridge, where they found the arch sprung, and went hard to work to repair it. Before this was effected the main body had arrived, and the moment the passage was practicable, all moved over and marched on through the night, until the sight of bivouac fires on the height and in the valley about Amsteg, induced them to halt for daylight.

On the 26th, the moment objects could be distinguished, shouts of welcome broke forth alike from the soldiers on the height, and the column which hurried on to greet their comrades; who at once were recognised to be Auffenberg's battalions. This good officer and his men—Austrians all—had done their duty nobly.

★★★★★★

Note:—Can any soldier traverse these glorious scenes without envying these gallant men! Dumas well describes how vividly the "*gaudia certaminis*" must have been heightened among them: "*La guerre de montagnes est (si l'ou veut nous passer cette expression) la partie poetique de l'art de la guerre. Les forces physiques y sont continuellement exercées, et les forces morales n'y sont pas moins exaltées. Si l'air qu'on respire dans ces hautes régions raffermit les nerfs, donne au corps plus d'agilité, les idées sont aussi plus nettes, l'esprit est plus fécond en ressources, le courage est toujours audacieux, les mouvemens sont prompts, les actions décisives, tout est vif, brillant, et rapide; aussi voit-on d'ordinaire ceux qui ont fait la guerre dans les montagnes fort épris de leur métier parcequ'ils y ont trouvé—helas! comme les chasseurs, avec de grands dangers des jouissances plus vives: et peut-être que les parfums de l'Asie brulant devant le char de triomphe du vainqueur de Darius, lui causèrent moins de joie que n'en crut avoir le Général Lecourbe, lorsqu'il rencontra sur les bords des précipices de la Reuss les colonnes qui avaient franchi les glaces du Saint Gothard."*

★★★★★★

Reaching the Maderanerthal, after their toilsome march late on the 24th, they had halted some hours at the strong ground by the Ezli fall; and, descending on Amsteg at day break next morning, had suddenly fallen on the enemy occupying it, and driven him down the valley. Reinforced from Altorf, he returned 2,000 strong, and made every exertion to recover the bridge over the Kerstenen torrent, on which Lecourbe depended for his retreat: but utterly in vain; Auffenberg repulsing him and again driving him back towards Altorf. Scarcely, however, was this done when Lecourbe's 6,000 men came pouring down the road from Wasen; and, facing about to meet them, Auffenberg long maintained the strong and rugged ground, commanding in front and rear the important point he had seized with glorious pertinacity.

But Lecourbe, with a superiority of three to one, was a man not to be denied, when the fate of his column rested on the winning of the bridge. While the greater portion of his force maintained an incessantly superior fire upon the Austrians, pressing them up the lower falls and ledges of the Breitenstoch, he himself, at the head of a selected column, went right upon the bridge and won and held it. Auffenberg retired fighting, up the height that overlooked it, and maintaining the strong gorge of the Maderanerthal; from which Lecourbe vainly endeavoured to dislodge him, till apprehensive of the appearance of Suwarow in his own rear, he, as soon as the bridge which he had fired had burned sufficiently, continued his retreat on Altorf.

The instant the Russians had joined their comrades, their united advance passed along the still burning beams of the Kerstenen bridge and pushed on for Altorf; which, after repulsing parties of the enemy near Erstfeld, at the Schachen bridge by Burglen, and at Attinghausen, they entered at noon. Lecourbe's force had crossed the Reuss and occupied the ground on its left by Seedorf, of which they held the bridge; Suwarow's main body bivouacked by the Schachen bridge; Rosenberg and Auffenberg occupying Altorf; but the rear of the column of march, retarded by the various obstacles, was still at

111

Suwarow crossing the Alps

some distance, covered by detachments posted at the lateral valleys, and Strauch's Austrians, who had remained on the St. Gothard.

★★★★★★

Note:—The old landlord of the "Eagle," at Altorf, came with Suwarow from Italy as one of his guides; and though the poor old gentleman is now so aged as to remember but confusedly what he saw so long ago, he has two very amusing pictures of the actions in the Muttenthal, done by himself soon after the events, which he willingly shows his guests.

★★★★★★

The French having naturally secured all the boats on the Lucerne Lake, Suwarow's only mode of reaching Schwyz was by the Senner's or Cattle-people's path over the Kinzigkulm, the steep and lofty ridge which runs between the Schachen and Muttenthal; and early on the 27th, Bagration's advance led the way along the path which to this day is pointed out with interest by the people as "the Russians road." The difficulties and sufferings of this march far exceeded those of any as yet made by the main body of the army. The ascent is continuous and very stiff for near 5,000 feet, and parts of the descent are as rugged as they well can be to be passable. For much of the way the men had to move in single file, dragging themselves and their animals along the rude and often undistinguishable paths over crags and boggy ground; and here and there by precipices dangerous to an animal, and not pleasant even to men accustomed to these mountain tracks.

But worst of all (and indeed, throughout this wondrous operation, this was the most serious, painful, and insuperable of all the difficulties encountered), the troops, as well as their mules and horses, were weak for want of proper sustenance. And to this sad fact, far more than to any real difficulty in this march, (which is in truth simply a stiff mountain walk of six or at most seven hours,) must it be ascribed that so many of the men and beasts sank down and died in the course of it, as to give rise to the romantic legend of the peasants, mentioned by M. Simond, that the birds of prey grew dainty, and fed their young ones only with the eyes of the corpses. It is said that none of the corps took less than twelve or fourteen hours to do this march.

At about a mile from Mutten, which is there completely screened from view by the woods and rocks which almost wall in the valley, a path goes left and descends below the village; and by this. Bagration detached a party to intercept the enemy's retreat on Schwyz, and then descending with his main body, fell suddenly and unexpectedly on the surprised companies stationed in the valley, and killed or captured every man of them. While the head of the army was thus employed, and Suwarow with its centre following Bagration, the rear was sharply attacked at Altorf by Lecourbe; but Rosenberg successfully repulsed him and drove him back over the Seedorf bridge.

Early, however, on the morning of the 28th, the indefatigable Lecourbe again fell on the Russian rear-guard, as the long line of baggage passed up the Schachenthal under its protection; and when this had gained sufficient way, Rosenberg once more by a gallant dash pushed back his persevering enemies, and then slowly following the train, which wound upwards from the valley to the ridge of the Kinzigkulm, covered it so long as the enemy continued a straggling pursuit; and afterwards, passing It at the Seenalp pastures, descended on Mutten which he entered late at night.

Here, on the previous day, Suwarow had learnt that Masséna, anticipating his intentions, had on the 25th September, attacked Korsakow and the Allies, completely beaten them, and driven them from the Linth and Limmat to the Rhine. He thus found himself in a chasm of the Alps, the mountains he had passed, behind him; Mount Bräghel to his right, the Mythen chain in front, and the lake and Schwyz upon his left, all occupied by a victorious enemy; his friends routed, and his army wearied, wasted, and starving: their shoes cut from their feet; their provisions exhausted, and their ammunition almost expended. But we see no change in the dauntless bearing of the brave old man. He wrote to Korsakow and the other generals:—

Your heads shall answer it if you fall back another step. I am coming to remedy your blunders. I shall show no favour, so stand like walls.

To cut his way to them, by Schwyz, through the heart of the French Army, was his first idea; but the uncertainty of their position rather than the hazard of the measure, inducing him to relinquish It. He resolved to force Mount Bräghel and the Klönthel, and march on Glaris; whence roads branch off to Wasen and Wallenstadt, by which he hoped to communicate with the left of the beaten army. His troops halted on the 29th, except Auffenberg's brigade, which marched on that day to secure Mount Bräghel and advance towards Glaris. Beyond a doubt the men much needed rest; but it seems evident, in the gaiety affected by Suwarow, and in the ostentatious exhibition of his baggage and his military orders, which were all unpacked and paraded to be aired, that he was pleased with the opportunity this necessity afforded of showing how coolly he encountered the calamities that beset him.

On the 30th, he reported his position and intentions to the Emperor Francis; stating that on the 29th, he had received from General Linken the disagreeable news of the defeat the army had sustained at Zurich, in consequence of which the operations for the general attack on this side would have to be given up, and that as he had heard that Linken had been checked at Glaris he had despatched Auffenberg to join him. He concludes:—

The more distressing all this is, the more shall I exert myself to keep the enemy from any further attempts, and to unite myself with the Imperial troops.

In pursuance of this object, leaving Rosenberg with his division at Mutten to protect his rear and the passage of the baggage, he, with the main body, on the 30th joined Auffenberg; who, after carrying Mount Bräghel, had been checked in the Klönthal. The enemy now reinforced, and under the command of General Molitor, occupied the lower end of the valley in front of its lake; the narrow path along which, in their rear, ran for full two miles between steep heights on one side and deep water on the other, and was not only obstructed by abattis and rude traverses, but at its lower end for a good half-mile was completely swept by the French artillery, from as pretty a small defensive position as eye could look on. General Molitor on being summoned to surrender, replied that he had defeated General Jellachich on the 26th and 27th, and General Linken on the 28th and 29th, and in his turn recommended the Russians to lay down their arms, as Masséna at Schwyz closed up the Muttenthal behind them.

★★★★★★

Note:—The defence of the Linthal, by Molitor, is amongst the most perfect studies with which the annals of war present us. Another not less admirable is Lecourbe's attack on the St. Gothard, on the 15th August. It is impossible to suppress a thrill of honest pride in recollecting that our national glories have been won from these heroic men; and it is no unimportant corollary to such recollections, to bear in mind that our national independence and honour has to be defended against their like.

★★★★★★

Dispositions to fall on the enemy in front and on his right flank, having been made, Suwarow told the men the enemy had desired them to surrender, and pointing first to the Archduke Constantino who rode beside him, and then to the hostile ranks, gave the word for battle, when all pressed onward with a general shout. The flank attack was so ardent as to cause almost immediate confusion, and in spite of all Molitor's exertions, after a brave resistance, the French were beaten back, and so borne into and along the pathway by the lake, that both its strong defences and the admirable ground beyond, were passed by the Russians intermingled with them; nor was the struggle and pursuit down the valley of the Lontech arrested till darkness precluded further movement on such uncertain ground. As it was, one sharp turn where the road forms a step or ledge between the Weggis mountain, and the deep chasm of the Lontech, is still pointed out as the spot where a number of both parties, in the dusk of the evening, went headlong over the precipice and were dashed to pieces,—the appalling screams of those upon the brink being lost amid the savage shout of the pursuers, who in a few seconds lay silently beside them.

With the morning of the 1st of October, the action recommenced, and after defending their ground bravely to Netsthal—the bridge beyond which over the Linth they burnt, "not without difficulty," as Molitor reports, "the Russians mixing with them and fighting only with the bayonet"—the French fell back on the villages of Mollis and Näfels; where they enjoyed no longer respite from attack than till the Russians had replaced the Netsthal bridge by a temporary one on trestles. But Gazan's (late Soult's) division joined them in these villages, from Wasen, and turned the scale of numbers in their favour.

The chief object of the Allies in their renewed attack was to possess themselves of Mollis, from which the path mounts the Kerenzenberg to Wallenstadt; and more especially the bridge over the Linth beyond it, leading to Näfels and Wasen. But the strength of this post, comprising a long defile and village, closed in between the mountains and the river, and completely overlooked and commanded by the strong height beyond it—under the retired right flank of which stands the bridge, open alike to their fire and to every support that could be sent from the other side the Linth, and maintained not only by Molitor's good soldiers, but by the reinforcements and guns which continued to arrive throughout the day from Wasen—completely baffled the desperate attacks of Bagration's weak force; and, after penetrating on either side the river to Näfels and Mollis, (to the latter, and even to its bridge, it is asserted, six several times) the Russians were withdrawn at ten at night, and took post at Netsthal; Suwarow and headquarters being at Glaris.

While the leading column of the Russian Army had been thus engaged, on the 30th September and 1st October, its rear division under Rosenberg, at Mutten, had signalised each of these days by separate defeats of the enemy led on by Masséna in person. After a reconnoissance up the Schachenthal on the 29th, this general, having returned to Brunnen by the lake, moved with some thousands of Mortier's division up the Muttenthal on the 30th, and at two p.m. attacked the Russian outposts; which gradually fell back on two *Jäger* battalions, whose resistance had already seriously engaged the enemy; when three fresh battalions breaking through the line of fire, came fiercely on with the bayonet, supported by a general hurrah of the Cossacks, who charged through the Muttenbach on the scattered infantry. The French gave way, and were closely followed halfway to Schwyz, losing a gun and several hundred men; of whom many were dashed into the Muttenbach chasm, which for some distance yawns beside the road in the narrowest part of the wild and beautiful defile through which they fled. At night the Russians were led back to Mutten: except Velesky's regiment, which remained in observation down the valley.

It may easily be conceived that Masséna exerted all his influence to excite his men to obliterate the disgrace of this discomfiture; and next morning they advanced with reinforced numbers, amounting to near 10,000 men and a strong force of artillery, with the intent to do so. At eleven in the morning they opened their fire on Velesky's men, who fell back in order, and with slight resistance; till on nearing Mutten they filed off to either flank, and displayed a line of three battalions, stretching across the narrow valley just below the village, where a jutting rock and the Muttenbach beneath it secured their right flank, with a second line of five battalions in their rear.

The 1st October was the Emperor Paul's birthday; and nobly did his soldiers illustrate it, by one of the most splendid, rapid, and decisive exhibitions of their simple battle tactics, which history records. Regardless alike of the superior numbers of the enemy and the fire of their artillery, at the word of their worthy general, they dashed on headlong, with their bayonets at the charge, and by this simple effort overthrew at once all order in the enemy's masses; and, driving them into a flying mob, pursued them unremittingly, without affording them time to recover themselves, down the whole course of the Mutten valley and defile, over the Steinernebrücke and its awful chasm, and up and down the height of Schönenbach, even to the farther side of Schwyz and Brunnen, a distance of full ten English miles.

From 1,000 to 1,500 prisoners, with five cannon, were the trophies of this distinguished feat of arms. Great numbers of the French were killed and wounded, and hurried on and pitched into the Muttenbach chasm; and so completely had they dispersed themselves, in their dismay, up the difficult heights which shut in the valley, that those who came straggling down to Schwyz for two or three days after the action, are described as having escaped *"par des sentiers et des votes impossibles!"*

When the victorious Russians, after their long and ardent pursuit, once more resumed their ground at Mutten, Masséna, in despair of doing anything with them on this ground, blew up the Steinernebrücke, to keep them in the valley; and, leaving two demi-brigades to observe them, moved the remainder of his force by Einsiedeln to Wasen, and the entrance to the Linthal: and this (*par parenthese*) was good sound strategy; for even had he beaten Rosenberg out of the Muttenthal, he would have forced him back upon Suwarow, and thus united their forces; whereas could he have pushed Suwarow back from Glaris before their junction, Rosenberg and his men would have been isolated and surrounded on every side.

★★★★★★

Note:—Count M. Dumas (*Précis des Evênemens Militaires*) says: "Suwarow was marching on Schwyz when attacked by Masséna on the 4th October, but being repulsed, he turned on Molitor at Glaris." The date is probably a misprint, but the statement is utterly erroneous; and we find Suwarow, so soon after the event as the 21st November, replying in the *Augsburg Gazette* to Masséna's report, and distinctly stating that "it was well known 3,000 Russians had completely defeated 10,000 picked men, at the head of whom Masséna had rashly attacked them in the Muttenthal, and that the Republicans lost their cannon." It is certain that the advance of his army was engaged in the Klonthal, and beyond Glaris, on the 29th and 30th September and 1st October; and we cannot suppose even Suwarow so desperate, had he resolved to debouche into the midst of a victorious army by Schwyz, as to seek to do so with the rearguard only of his force. From the moment Auffenberg marched on the Bräghel, all idea of moving by Schwyz was given up, and Rosenberg was at Mutten (when attacked by Masséna) to protect the passage of the baggage; which, during the whole period of his stay there, continued to pass on to Glaris by the Bräghel.

★★★★★★

At Glaris, Suwarow had found some provisions, but so scanty was the supply, that his men were seen raking the very dung-heaps, to discover anything eatable.

The strength of the pass of Mollis—by the knowledge that the enemy was in great force at Wasen, and the absolute uncertainty whether they or the Austrians were at Wallenstadt, added to the utter exhaustion of his ammunition, determined Suwarow to effect his movement to the Rheinthal by the Sernfthal and Panix. His sick, wounded, and baggage commenced their march on the afternoon of the 4th Oct., on which day Rosenberg's division arrived at Glaris from Mutten, and on the 5th the fighting men left Glaris. The rear of the army was harassed by the French, whom Bagration vigorously repulsed with the bayonet at Schwanden. They, however, continued their pursuit as far as Matt; where, finding the Russians steadily in position and themselves much inconvenienced by a heavy fall of snow, which seemed inclined to last, they relinquished any further pursuit, and returned to Glaris.

This snow was a dreadful aggravation of the difficulties the Russians had to encounter and endure in the march before them, over a most rugged Alpine pass of 7,500 feet in height, and they continued to drop along its whole extent in melancholy numbers. Famine and fatigue had quite exhausted them; though perhaps the presence of their enemies might have stimulated many to active exertion, who sank down despairingly to die along the toilsome paths of the Jatzalp and Rinkenkopf. Their light guns and those they had captured were buried; most of the beasts of burthen had died, or were abandoned; crowds of sick and wounded gave themselves up amid the driving snows that beat in their faces and accumulated round them; and it was the 10th October, before the last of the lame, maimed, and spectral relics of this army of heroes descended in the Rheinthal.

Suwarow and the advance entered Panix late on the 6th. On reaching Ilantz on the 7th, he met General Linken, one of those whose conduct had so increased his difficulties. "General Linken," he said, in his abrupt manner, "how many Frenchmen have your fellows spitted on their bayonets? Mine have had six a piece."

The general promptly replying, "My men do their best, sir; and they do well."

Suwarow, pleased with his answer, held out his hand. The actual loss of the Russians was little more than 3,000 men, but the condition and destitution of the army was indescribable. Still the most worn and suffering soldier had his pride of heart and sense of duty to reconcile him to the present, and to brighten the prospects of the future. But not so the wretched inhabitants of the valleys through which this "living cloud of war" had held its course: they were utterly undone; for though discipline had been observed (and the Russian is a kindly being) the urgent necessities of the army had actually extorted everything consumable, just at the beginning of the winter, and the population of whole villages had to descend from their native valleys to commence a life of beggary or exile.

Thus, terminated the march by the St. Gothard—a memorable example of soldierly exertion, intrepidity, and endurance; the glories of which will live in prominent and singular brilliancy, as the sole relief to the shameful disgrace and ruin resulting from the combination of which it was a part. Mons. Thiers concludes his relation of these events thus:—"*Ce barbare, prétendu invincible, se retirait convert de cojifusion et plein de rage;*" while the very opposite sentiment "*Je donnerais toutes mes campagnes pour celle de la Suisse du Maréchal Suwarow,*" has been given by another French historian as the eulogium of Moreau and Masséna upon them.

CHAPTER 5

Previous Events in Switzerland

Suwarow was now made fully acquainted with the occurrences of the 25th September. Korsakow having posted 10,000 men in detached bodies on the right of the Limmat, at and below Zurich, and 14,000 on its left bank, within the arc formed by it and the lake, had been attacked by Masséna; who passed 15,000 men across the river at Dietiken, beat the detachments, and seized the Schaffhausen and Winterthur roads, while the remainder of his army defeated the Russian main body. During the night, after losing 6,000 men, the whole Russian force was united in Zurich—the French commanding every road leading from it, but that to Rapperschwyl, Uznach, Wasen, &c. If determined to win or die, Korsakow could have thrown his collected force on one or other divisions of his enemy's army. If to unite with the Austrians and Suwarow, he might have left a garrison in Zurich, and effected this object by marching early in the night along an open road.

He remained, however, stationary till morning, and then led his men to cut their way through Masséna's victorious troops, to march on Bulach and Schaffhausen: his infantry in front, then his cavalry, and lastly, his baggage and artillery. His brave infantry forced their way through all opposition with no very great loss: in fact, so long as they fought, they were conquering; the cavalry naturally suffered more, and all the guns and materials fell into the hands of the enemy. But if every soldier he commanded had been cut to pieces, it would not have been more immediately injurious to the cause he served than was his choice of direction in his retreat. He went north.

★★★★★★

Note:—Had he fallen back on Rapperschwyl, the road to which was open to him, he might have rallied to his army Petrasch and Jellachich; and, if unable to maintain himself at Wasen and the

121

mouth of the Linthal, have fallen back on the Rhine at Lucienberg and Maienfeld; or, at the very worst, have been driven to the river towards Feldkirch, against which position Masséna had already spilt the best blood of the army in vain, and whence he might have communicated or co-operated with Suwarow by Wallenstadt and the Kerengen.

Every principle of military combination, of brother soldierhood, and common-sense, every right feeling of the officer and man, alike indicated Rapperschwyl as the line of his retreat from Zurich. Soult's troops were no sufficient obstacles to deter him: they did not enter Rapperschwyl till the 26th, and then not in force. He might have gained six or eight hours' march on Masséna; and the brave men he sacrificed (who, by every version, fought, while they were allowed to do so, with perfect desperation) would doubtless have done the rest for him. But he seemed entirely divested of all self-possession. He compromised one gallant army by his blind presumption, and another by his eagerness to escape its consequences.

★★★★★★

Soult easily defeated Hotze's force, their leader falling at the beginning of the action, and General Petrasch, who succeeded him, led his beaten people utterly unpursued due east, as far as Rheineck; while Generals Linken and Jellachich allowed themselves to be driven from the Linthal by a single brigade, numbering scarce a third of their united force. All were disgracefully defeated, and all retreated eccentrically, and from Suwarow, whom they knew was advancing into the midst of the enemy's army, in undoubting confidence of their zealous co-operation. Had they deliberately conspired for his ruin, no one of them could have done more than he did to effect it.

Wearied as Suwarow's men must have been on reaching Ilantz on the 7th, their earnest chief, knowing it was still in the enemy's power to interrupt his junction with Petrasch and Korsakow, by seizing upon Maienfeld, marched all his effective men on the 8th to Coire, and joining Jellachich occupied Maienfeld. On the 11th the Russians marched to Balzers, and on the 12th to Feldkirch. Here Suwarow, having united himself to the wreck of the Austrian left of the Allied Army of Switzerland, informed the Archduke Charles (who with his army had arrived at Stockach) that he proposed to march against the enemy on the 17th by Alstetten, on St. Gall and Winterthur; that Korsakow was to pass the Rhine by Stein, and join him by Pfyn and Frauenfeld, and Condé to do so from Constance, by Bischofszell and Wyl; praying the archduke to support the latter, and to co-operate personally, in case of the movement, in such way and degree as he thought fit.

Receiving no immediate answer to his proposition from the archduke, and hearing from those around him that he showed no signs of preparing for co-operation, Suwarow on the 14th resolved to march his own force round the Constance Lake to join with Korsakow's. He communicated this his decision to the archduke, on receiving from His Highness, not a promise to support him as required, but a critique on his projected operation, with His Highness's correction thereof, substituting the movement of Korsakow to join Suwarow by Stockach, and the back of the lake of Constance.

Soured by his reverse (the first great cause of which he knew to be the archduke's march to Germany), and irritated at the unseemly interference of this young and methodical general in his plans, he became convinced that it was hopeless to think of operations based on co-operation between them; and to use his own expression, "having lost all hope in the archduke," he on reaching Lindau on the 16th, declared that his men were so exhausted, and so destitute of shoes, ammunition, and other necessaries, that for the present they were incapable of pursuing active operations, and insisted on placing them in quarters of refreshment: and here virtually ended Suwarow's participation in the events of the campaign. It should be strongly borne in mind that the general operation of the union of the army from Italy with that in Switzerland, was not a plan of Suwarow's, but peremptorily ordered by the Vienna cabinet in despite of his remonstrance; and that its security mainly depended on the maintenance of things *in statu quo* in Switzerland until it should have been effected.

It is evident that the departure of so large a force of Austrians under the Archduke Charles from Switzerland, before the arrival there of the Russians from Italy (contrary to the pledges of the Austrian cabinet to the courts of Russia and England, and in disregard of Suwarow's strong remonstrance), left the safety of Korsakow's army dependent on the gross improbability that Masséna would stand still with his superior army, for a month, before an unknown general and inferior force, stretched out from Dissentis in the Rheinthal to the confluence of the Aar and Rhine, to await his destruction in the junction of the best troops and most dreaded leader of the Coalition. Korsakow owed the respite he enjoyed after the archduke's departure, to the fame of the army he so thoughtlessly abandoned. The French Minister of War had written to Masséna, he says:—

To sustain and if necessary, excite the emulation of corps. In action against the Russians, take the most deeply weighed precautions; strike in masses, and have reserves to restore the battle when required. It is essential that in your first action against them you gain the advantage, so as to give the necessary confidence to our troops and to lower the pride of these semi-barbarians.

Anxiety to assemble and perfect all his means, delayed Masséna till he heard Condé and Bavarian reinforcements were near Schaffhausen, when he fixed his attack for the 26th, and on Suwarow's approach advanced it to the 25th. It was masterly in itself, and the misconduct of the Allied Generals made it decisive. Suwarow's previous arrival could alone have prevented the catastrophe, and that it was not so prevented would have been, perhaps, attributable to his choice of route; were it not that the delay in the supply of mules by the Austrian commissariat, which irremediably sacrificed five days, would have rendered it impossible for Suwarow to have joined Korsakow, even by the unoccupied Splugen or Bernardine road, so as to have anticipated Masséna's attack upon him.

Still, as this delay was accidental and unforeseen, Suwarow must be considered fairly amenable to the valid objections that may be adduced against his preference of the hazardous road by the St. Gothard to the open and easier one by the Splugen, in an operation whose realization depended more on time than anything else. By the St. Gothard he proposed to join Hotze, who commanded the left of the Allied Army in Switzerland, at Einsiedeln, by the Splugen; he would have joined him at Wasen, and the number of marches required to place him at Bellinzona in the first case, would have taken him to Riva at the head of the lake of Como in the other. The distances and difficulties from each of these points to their respective goals are as follows:—

BY THE ST. GOTHARD.

From Bellinzona to Airolo	.	10 leagues—slight ascent.
	OCCUPIED IN FORCE BY THE ENEMY.	
„ Airolo to Summit	. .	2 leagues—steep ascent.
„ Summit to Altorf	. .	10 leagues—descent and level.
„ Altorf to Mutten	. .	7 leagues—very stiff ascent and descent.
„ Mutten to Schwyz	. .	3 leagues—level.
„ Schwyz to Einsiedeln	.	3 leagues—very stiff ascent by Haken, or 4 leagues by Rothenthurm.

35 leagues.

From Riva to Chiavenna . . 3 leagues—level road.
„ Chiavenna to Summit . 6 leagues—ascent.
„ Summit to Coire . . 13 leagues—descent and level.
„ Coire to Wallenstadt . 8 leagues—level road.
„ Wallenstadt to Wasen . 5 leagues—hilly march by
                    Kerenzen, or 4 leagues
                    by lake.
                    ——
                    35 leagues.

By the St, Gothard from Altorf to Mutten, there was no road; and on this line are the three ascents of the St. Gothard, the Kinzighulm, and the Haken. The Splugen road was all good; the ascent of the mountain graduated for a long distance, and as the Allies held the lake of Wallenstadt, it is probable that the infantry alone would have had to cross the Kerenzen hill. By the St. Gothard, the army would have to carry its provisions for every inch of the way: by the Splugen, only for the one or two days passed between the two large towns of Chiavenna and Coire.

As is shown, the St. Gothard line was held by the enemy from Airolo. None but friends were on, or near the Splugen. The junction at Einsiedeln not only required an uninterrupted series of successes on Suwarow's side, but the carrying of the strong position of the Etzch by Hotze, who was nervously distrustful of the power of the force he commanded to maintain even its defensive position on the Linth; and it was evident that the moment Suwarow reached Airolo, or probably Faido, intelligence of the event would naturally be sent to Masséna, so as to enable him to attempt his worst on Hotze or Korsakow before the junction. The junction at Wasen required only that things should remain *in statu quo*; and Hotze's position there so far co-operated towards this result, that, interposing himself as he did between the enemy and what would have been the line of Suwarow's approach, it is more than probable Masséna would have been kept in perfect ignorance of it.

As the point of departure for an enemy advancing by the western side of the Zurich lake to turn Mount Albis, and push a force occupying it into the angles formed by the confluence of the Limmat, Reuss, and Aar, the sole difference between Einsiedeln and Wasen is, that the former is three leagues of strong ground, the latter six of open, from Richterschwyl, where their respective roads converge. As regards the possibility of previous reverse to the Allies in Switzerland, such as happened, the army moving on Einsiedeln is compromised, and at best

125

has to fight its way from among its enemies; while a force moving on Wasen by the Splugen, would, in its daily marches, rally to itself all that had fled to or near to the Rheinthal: which, as results turned out, would have included the entire Austrian force in Switzerland.

No admirer of Suwarow will doubt for a moment but that, had he taken the Splugen road, and had things happened precisely as they did, he would have been able to restore them by falling on Masséna's scattered left, with the force (near 40,000 men), he would have had in hand on reaching Wallenstadt. But he chose what we must suppose he considered a more brilliant task, and thus risked the fate of Switzerland, the spell of his own invincibility, and the existence of his noble army, on a most desperate and unnecessary chance. Our admiration of the manner in which he discharged his share of its duties, in no decree extenuates the error of his choice. His first duty was to secure the safety of the common cause, by those means which involved least chance of failure; and, while the Archduke Charles unquestionably created the dangers which threatened it, it is no less palpable that Suwarow, in striving to avert them, allowed himself to be allured from the easiest and quickest way of doing it.

The Russian officer with whose relation Jomini presents us, disapproves both of the St. Gothard and the Splugen; pronouncing that Suwarow should have crossed the Great St. Bernard, and entered the Pays de Vaud, forty leagues in rear of the French Army. He seems to have Marengo in his head: but Suwarow had not numbers to justify the movement. The weakness of their respective corps made union the first object of the Allies; and any combination was proportionally bad or good as it left their separated bodies an hour more or less exposed to attack by their superior enemy. Provided Suwarow left him time to annihilate Korsakow, it mattered little to Masséna where he entered Switzerland with 18,000 men. Three to one are sufficient odds, even against the Russians and "their father."

The political baseness of Austria—made manifest to Europe by the Articles of the Peace of Campo Formio, wherein she consented to accept the territories of Venice, her Italian ally, as the price of her betrayal of her German countrymen and supporters—and now consistently followed up by her present intention of appropriating to herself the Italian conquests, which Paul desired to restore to their legitimate owners; had created in Suwarow's mind a deep distrust towards her leading men; while the methodical slowness and inefficiency of the Archduke Charles's military proceedings, associated with His Highness's very ill-judged and indelicate habit of suggestive correspondence, exhibited a deficiency of perfect cordiality and earnestness (to Suwarow's single-mindedness almost equivalent to honesty) of purpose, which ill prepared either party to act as co-operative restorers of the calamitous condition of affairs in Switzerland.

The Austrian prince was known to undervalue what he considered the barbarian energy of the Russian leader, as unscientific; and Suwarow too openly scoffed at His Highness's pedantic estimation of rules and methods of war, which had so often led to disaster and defeat; and which, in truth, were far more opposite to just principles than his own death-or victory system. The reverse in Switzerland, involving at once the defeat of Korsakow and the pusillanimous retreats of the Austrian generals, aggravated their misunderstanding, by furnishing matter of mutual recrimination.

Still, though the archduke strongly felt (and in his later writings has since displayed) much of the professional and patriotic prejudice which estranged the Allies, he showed himself at this period most anxious to re-establish matters on a friendly footing: but in vain. His unfortunate reply to Suwarow's proposal to advance on the enemy from Feldkirch, combining at once a pretension to correct the old general's military views, and a postponement, if not evasion, of the operation he contemplated, filled to overflowing the cup of bitterness which Austria had mixed for him. Giving up all hope of restoring matters, Suwarow found at once indulgence and justification in aggravating the incidents of the cruel retrospect, to which he wholly turned. He spoke incessantly of the pledges given him, by the infraction of which his army had been baffled and exposed to ruin.

He saw in Austria a faithless ally—in her prince a treacherous rival. After witnessing the bravery and skill of the Austrian officers in Italy, he could see nothing but disloyalty and design in the deficiencies of those in Switzerland; and we can scarcely wonder, when the fortuitous concurrence of circumstances was such as to mislead dispassionate contemporaries, that Suwarow regarded this in the light of a systematic conspiracy to defraud him of his glory.

★★★★★★

Note:—Even at the present day (1846) we read the following passage in the pages of one of the honestest, if not the most correct, of French historians, Mons. Capefigue:—"*Mais qui peut expliquer l'inaction de l'Archiduc Charles laissant battre les Russes, tandis que deux de ses divisions pouvaient rétablir l'égalité, la balance*

*des forces, et donner la victoire aux Allies? C'est que, il faut bien le
dire, le Cabinet de Vienne était fort aise de voir les idées, les plans de
la cour Russe, et les forces Russes en dehors de toute action, politique
et militaire: on s'en était servi pour assurer l'évacuation de l'Italie par
les Français, pour gagner les batailles; mais maintenant qu'on voulait
négocier, l'influence de Paul était de trop. On ne faisait pas écraser les
forces de Suwarow, mais on les laissait exposées aux corps de Masséna;
et l'on vit plus d'un sourire sous les tentes Autrichiennes, à l'aspect de
ces leçons données par Masséna au presomptueux Korsakow."*

★★★★★★

He pertinaciously declined an interview with the archduke; and, at
length, when an officer of the prince's staff, Count Colloredo, waited
on him at Lindau with some proposition of a defensive nature, the
bitterness of his feelings broke out in his reply, he said:—

Tell my lord the prince, that I know nothing of the defensive;
I can only attack. I shall advance when it seems good to me
to do so; and when I do, I shall not stop in Switzerland. I shall
go, according to my orders, into Franche Comté. Tell him, that
at Vienna I am at his feet, but that here I am at least his equal.
He is a field-marshal, so am I; he serves a great emperor, so do
I; he commands an army, so do I; he is young, and I am old. I
have acquired experience by successive victories; and I receive
neither counsel nor advice from any one: I trust alone in God
and my sword.

Pressed alike by the English and Austrian envoys to become more
tractable, he answered:—

I left Italy sooner than I ought, in conformity to a plan which I
adopted in confidence on others, not from my own conviction.
I arrange my march into Switzerland—I send my route—I pass
the St. Gothard, and all the obstacles that present themselves—
I arrive, at the appointed day, on the spot where we were to
unite—and all fail me at once. Instead of finding an army in
good order in an advantageous position, I find no army at all.
The position of Zurich, which should have been defended by
60,000 Austrians, had been left to 20,000 Russians, and they allowed to want provisions. Hotze lets himself be surprised. Korsakow causes himself to be beaten. The French are masters of
Switzerland: and I find myself alone, with my troops without
artillery, provisions, or ammunition, obliged to retire into the

Grisons to join a routed army. Nothing has been done that was promised me. An old soldier like me may be taken in once, but he would be too great a fool to be so twice. I cannot again enter into a plan of operations from which I see no advantage. I have sent a courier to St. Petersburgh. I shall rest my army; and I shall do nothing without the orders of my sovereign.

To this outbreak succeeded an active but totally resultless correspondence between the two leaders; in which Suwarow, having, on the 22nd, stated that His Highness's march out of Switzerland had put everything there into confusion, the archduke replied:—

> The departure of the troops out of Switzerland to Germany was in conformity to my destination, and could not create the least embarrassment there. The corps of 20,000 men, under Hotze, continued to hold its position in one part of Switzerland; and in the other, the relief of the Royal Imperial troops was effected by the Imperial Russian forces, under General Korsakow, in a position offering every military advantage, as agreed upon by that general on the 28th August. The peculiar embarrassments, however, occurred at a later period; particularly on the 25th September. Eyewitnesses have but one voice, or those who understand war but one opinion, on the subject; and in the French papers there is an enumeration of the enemy's forces at the period, which puts the matter beyond all question.

The special pleading of this document, in which the archduke glances so cavalierly over the grand point of the amount of force left by him in Switzerland—on which all Europe then, and his own opinion since, have pronounced him faulty—was little calculated to smooth Suwarow's ruffled temper: neither were his vague professions of a willingness to adopt the offensive, unaccompanied by any specific plan or declaration as to the degree to which his army should co-operate; his total silence on the subject of the ammunition and supplies which Suwarow required from him; or his almost insulting proposal that Suwarow would undertake the defence of his flank from Bassadingen to Petershausen with 10,000 men, while he attended to one of those exaggerated alarms from the middle Rhine, to which in this campaign he so repeatedly attached undue importance. Suwarow, however, did leave a portion of his forces under Rosenberg for a stated time near Bregentz, and on quitting Lindau with the remainder thus worded his *adieu* to His Highness:—

I march tomorrow to winter quarters between the Lech and Iller. The hereditary states must be defended as disinterested conquests ought to have been; *i.e.*, by acquiring the love of the people, by acting with justice; not by surrendering the Netherlands, nor by sacrificing two fine Italian Armies. An old soldier who has been near sixty years under arms, tells Your Highness this: a soldier who has led the armies of Joseph II. and Francis II. to victory, and placed Gallicia under the Austrian sceptre: a soldier who neither acts according to Demosthenic chatterings, nor to please Acamedicians, who only confuse sound thought: nor for the senate of Hannibal!

I am not a man of jealousies, demonstrations, countermarches, or the like: instead of such childishness, I trust to *coup d'oeil*, quickness, and energy. Although invaluable time for the liberation of Switzerland has been lost, it may yet be made up for. Let Your Royal Highness prepare with your whole army, exclusive of its detachments, for a speedy, energetic, and short winter campaign; make me acquainted with your plan, that we may understand each other; and I am ready, as soon as the roads are in a fit condition, to co-operate with the whole of my army with Your Highness, so that we may go body and soul together. .... In your letter you have used the word 'retreat' in reference to my movement. I must protest against this, and declare that in the whole course of my life I have had no more acquaintance with this word than with those of 'defensive war:' two words which at the opening of this present campaign have cost in the Tyrol alone 10,000 men; a loss as great as what Italy cost us.

I go solely to rest my people in winter quarters, to preserve them for the service of the two allied emperors, and to put them as quickly as possible in a condition to assist your Imperial Highness in the liberation of Switzerland; and, if Providence aid us, to pursue the liberation of the French kingdom from their oppressors.

A letter from Lindau, written the day after the archduke's officer had been with him, after describing Suwarow's half-shut eyes, single boot, embraces and benediction, gives the following account of the odd jumble of his conversation. The marshal observed:—

Some time ago, We only talked of victories and conquests; there is no more of that just now: unforeseen circumstances have made us change our tone; but it will come again, take my word for it. You will return to England, and see his Royal Highness the Count d'Artois; tell him our passage of the Alps equalled, if it did not surpass, that of Hannibal.

Then, turning to one of his *aides-de-camp*, he said:—

Tell the gentleman of our campaign, that he may give the details to His Royal Highness.

Then he continued to the company:—

The Romans said, that one ought to boast in public: it excites the emulation of the listeners.

After he had dined and asked some questions on affairs in Holland, with which he showed himself well acquainted, he proceeded:—

The English are fine fellows: they are a great people, and approach nearer than any others to angels.

He compared Ossian to Homer, and remarked that though the Romans called themselves the conquerors of the world, the Scotch had always successfully resisted them. He joked about roast beef, and after pressing Colonel Clinton to hurry the ale he had ordered for him, he turned the conversation on Rousseau: one of his generals observing he had written some excellent works, he said:—

Look at that *illuminé*, get out, you *illuminé!* Get out, you and your Rousseau!

Speaking with judgment on the harm done to religion by Voltaire, Jean Jacques, and Raynal. The general availing himself of a pause to say he meant Jean Baptiste Rousseau, not Jean Jaques, Suwarow replied, "Well, you may stay, as that's the case."
He spoke of his battles in Italy:—

Caesar said one should never *parley* with barbarians: they who call themselves our friends are often worse. What's the use of talking, writing, or communicating? When two men are friends, whether Russian, French, English, or German, this (putting his hand on his heart) speaks and directs both to the same end. Like Caesar, I make no partial plans. I look at things as a whole; for a whirlwind of events always changes plans that have been arranged.

He mentioned that an adjutant (who was present) had fallen, without being hurt, down a precipice, saying, "Do you know who saved him? It was the devil—he's a freemason."

After further conversation, he turned to the image of St. Nicholas, returned thanks, gave his blessing to the company, and retired to rest awhile, in the old cloak, which, at Lindau as elsewhere, was the bed of the *generalissimo* of the Russians. This title Suwarow had recently received from his sovereign, with an order that the same military honours should be paid him as to the emperor, even when that monarch should be present; and that he should be henceforth regarded as the greatest general of any age, people, or country.

Paul said, on issuing this order:—

This would be much for another, but it is little for Suwarow— he is more an angel than man!

It need not be here repeated that it is in no manner our object to assume for Suwarow the pride of place among martial heroes to which the *Czar* here elevates him. We hold him to be only a first rate general of a secondary class: still, so long as first class leaders shall be rare in war, the fate of nations may be confidently entrusted to such men as Suwarow and his soldiers. Their achievements in this campaign taxed the ingenuity of hostile historians to find terms in which to characterise them. The authors of *Les Victories, Conquetes, et Revers du Français*, say:—

Le héros de la Russie s'étoit crée un système de guerre propre à dé concerter par sa hizarrerie les combinaisnns savantes des tacticiens les plus expérimentés.

But the generals who compiled that work knew well that it is not the oddity of a system that gains success in war, but numbers, courage, combinations, and rapidity; and to the superior employment of one or other of these essentials, is due the praise thus ungenerously withheld from the military qualities of Suwarow.

The experienced tacticians of Austria, complained in terms not very dissimilar, of the odd and unaccommodating system adopted by Buonaparte, in his first Italian campaign. The Archduke Charles has lent his sanction to the depreciation of Suwarow; pronouncing him a man who would probably have done nothing without a superior force. It is no mean merit to have done what he did with one. We see the archduke himself taking ten weeks to advance from Stockach to Zurich, and then motionless for ten more in Switzerland; and eventually losing most important ground before he left it, with a proportionably stronger force available for attack than that with which the Russian leader baffled Moreau, Macdonald, and Joubert.

We do not claim for Suwarow the highest qualities of his art, but he had first-rate courage, activity, and decision: he could carry on his troops with an enthusiasm seldom equalled, and he fought desperately for victory. Defeat was unknown to him. He led the banners of Austria to a rapid succession of triumphs, to which its annals find no parallel; and he threw a glory over his march through Switzerland, which extorted the envy of his generous antagonists. This is something; and while the strategist sees in part of Suwarow's career an absence of the highest military qualifications, the soldier will feel proud to know what valour and energy can do; and, if he be wise, will seek those sources of knowledge which, had they been familiar to Suwarow, would have crowned his name with truer and more enduring glory.

At the end of October, Suwarow's headquarters were at Augsburg, whence his army broke up on the 23rd Nov. for Bohemia, where it was halted for final orders. The Emperor Paul had long suspected—when the representations of his son Constantino, of Suwarow, and above all, the evidence of unmistakeable facts convinced him—how opposite to the spirit of the coalition had been the policy and the proceedings of Austria. She had seized on Italy for herself; and now, in addition, he found one of his own brave armies sacrificed, by measures utterly at variance with the assurances she had given him.

★★★★★★

Note:—Immediately the news of the Archduke Charles's movement to Germany reached Paul, he indignantly and categorically demanded of the Austrian minister at his court (Coblentz), "On what grounds was the archduke's army so quickly to leave Switzerland, &c.?" He was momentarily pacified by the following precise explanation, to every word of which, events had already, a fortnight before it was written, practically given the lie:—"Baron Thugut has assured me that the Archduke Charles was to come to an understanding with the commander-in-chief of the Russian forces concerning the most proper ways and means of their march, so that the positions hitherto occupied by the armies of his Imperial Majesty should be one after another occupied by them, and thus the Austrian troops be relieved."

According to this, the Austrians were not otherwise to relinquish their positions than as successively relieved in them by the Russians as they advanced.

In the baron's despatch of the 22nd August, it is said, "that the relief is to commence by the substitution of Russians on the left of the line;" and, in the same despatch, it is particularly expressed that the archduke, in giving up these positions to the Russian troops, will occupy the remaining portion of the line till the arrival of the last Russian troops; and for the removal of every difficulty in regard to the Russian artillery and cavalry not then arrived, that Austrian artillery and cavalry shall be left till they came.

According to this, His Imperial Highness sees himself bound to remain with his army in Switzerland until the position of the Russian Army there be fully secured. With respect to the unfortunate events of the 15th August (the loss of the St. Gothard by the archduke's left wing), it is also said, "that His Imperial Majesty has given irrevocable orders to the Archduke Charles to employ all his forces to remedy this misfortune." After this, can it be supposed that the Austrian troops have left Switzerland in presence of the enemy, and before the relief by the Russian troops shall have been completely effected?

In addition to this, the "Intermediate Army is always to act in absolute co-operation with Field-Marshal Suwarow." So writes the diplomatist on the 13th September, whereas the Archduke Charles first communicates to Suwarow on the 29th August that he is about to leave Switzerland; and days before his letter has reached its destination, he is with his army, *already in Germany!* The sensation excited by this measure was not confined to Suwarow's army and the court of St. Petersburgh.

We find Woronzoff writing from London:—"The conduct of the council of war, with respect to the army of the Archduke Charles, has been heard here with astonishment. After this army had been kept in perfect inactivity for three months, thus giving time to Masséna to obtain all the reinforcements he could desire, it has been suddenly removed out of Switzerland—which it might have liberated, had it chosen to do so—leaving a small force of Russians at the mercy of the enemy, who outnumber them threefold!"

★★★★★★

In consequence, on the 22nd Oct., Paul had thus addressed the Emperor Francis:—

Your Majesty must already be aware of the consequence of the removal of your army under the Archduke Charles out of Switzerland, effected in defiance of all the motives for which it had remained there, to secure the union of the Army of Prince Italisky with General Korsakow. Seeing my troops deserted and delivered over to the enemy in this manner, and my views and the welfare of Europe sacrificed to a selfish policy, and having full cause for the indignation I feel at the conduct of your ministry (the motives of which I do not care to know), I declare to Your Majesty, with the same sincerity which led me to hasten to your assistance and to further the progress of your arms, that I from this day forth give up the common cause, in order that I may not lend myself to the triumph of a wicked one. I remain with the esteem due to you, &c., Paul.

It was in vain the Austrian court attempted to pacify him, sending one of the archdukes to St. Petersburgh, and doing all that could be done by words to reconcile him to the past: he was inexorable; demanding, as preliminaries to any restoration of their good understanding, that all the Austrian generals who commanded in Switzerland at the time of the Battle of Zurich should be brought to trial, that the Republic of Venice should be restored, and the King of Sardinia reestablished in his dominions.

Such terms were considered inadmissible by the Thugut cabinet; the second coalition was irrevocably dissolved, and Austria kept Italy till the following year; when Marengo, and subsequently Hohenlinden, inculcated, somewhat more convincingly than Paul had done, the wisdom of an honest policy. "Thus (in Suwarow's words) did the mountain produce its mouse." Instead of this, he asserts:—

Had the King of Sardinia been placed on his throne when the people were excited by our good conduct, an auxiliary army could have been raised as if by magic; and with the innumerable supplies of Turin, we might have been in Lyons by November, and at Paris with the new year. Liberation was our game, and justice—not *Indemnification!* That plays the game of the atheists, and serves them to drive you back again. Caesar said, 'I have done nothing till I have done all.' When you feel you hold the fate of France in your hands, seek and settle your indemnification in Paris. Just now your conquests are anything but secured. But then *Political Wisdom!* It was 'political wisdom' that gave away the Netherlands, and accepted Venice from Buonaparte for Lombardy. 'Political wisdom' is now even still more generous. It places Turin at Cagliari! Naples at Palermo! Won't it be wonderful some fine day to find Vienna at Presburg? Alas! alas! I am not the man, I find, to reconstruct the ruined fane of Themis!

On the 21st of January 1800, Suwarow's army was ordered to return to Russia; the field-marshal preceding them with a small suite, by Cracow and Wilna. At the former city he was attacked with illness, and subsequently lay many weeks ill at Kobrin; where Paul sent his own physician to attend him: writing:—

I pray to God to preserve my hero Suwarow. On reaching the capital you will experience the gratitude of Your Emperor; which, however, can never equal the good services you have done for me and for the Empire.

On leaving Wilna, Suwarow grew still worse, and was forced to remain some days in a peasant's hut near the road. Here he was heard more than once to exclaim, "Ah! I am become too old!" Still he struggled on, encouraged by the flattering reception prepared for him at St. Petersburgh; where Paul had arranged a triumphal military ceremony, which was to usher the old hero to the apartments allotted to him in the Imperial winter palace: which cheering promise was, however, to be cruelly disappointed.

It appeared that Paul had directed that the *generalissimo* should appoint a general of the day by roster, and that Suwarow had appointed, or allowed, Bagration (in whom he had most confidence,) to act permanently, or nearly so, as general of the day. Suwarow's enemies had represented the injustice of this in so strong a light to Paul, that the unfortunate man at once took the extreme step (without any communication whatever with Suwarow), of having It proclaimed at the head of every regiment in his service, that the *generalissimo*, Prince Italisky, having failed to comply with the Imperial commands, had merited severe censure.

Suwarow's strength of body and mind had of late been rapidly failing, and when he received intelligence of this event at Riga, the unexpected blow struck home, and aggravated all his ailments; he nevertheless continued his journey, and on the 2nd May, having purposely waited for nightfall, passed the barrier of St. Petersburgh at ten o'clock, and received in the "present" of the guard there, the last military honour of his life. Instead of to the Imperial Palace, he was carried to his nephew's hotel; where he lay down, never again to quit his bedroom. Here a few friends only ventured to visit him in secret.

The loss of his son was added to his other sufferings; and so rapidly was he sinking under his various miseries, that the extraordinary Paul relented, so far as to permit his friends to visit him, and to send a chamberlain to inquire after his health. Suwarow's eccentricity exhibited its last glimpse in receiving this person, whom Paul had ennobled when a menial servant, and in obstinately persisting in not recognising the badge of honour,—the blue ribband with which he was decorated,—but continuing to ask him what could have induced him to wear such a very fine waistcoat, interrupting him momentarily by exclaiming, "a blue waistcoat! why does the man wear a blue one?"

But he received the young archdukes very differently. To them he feelingly lamented what seemed to him the decline of the Empire, and regretted that his life had reached into such times. On the 17th May he received the sacrament, and next day an officer came to him from the emperor, to signify that His Majesty was graciously prepared to grant any request the *generalissimo* might wish to ask. One may well say with the poet, "Oh, cruel irony! this comes too late; and only mocks whom it was meant to honour." The message, however, seemed to summon Suwarow back to life: collecting the strength he had left, he raised himself on his couch and proceeded to enumerate one by one all the favours and honours he had received from the Empress Catherine, he said:—

I was nothing but a soldier full of zeal; but she felt the will I had to serve her. I owe her more than life, for she gave me the means of glorifying myself. Tell her son that I accept his Imperial promise. You see this portrait of the empress—it has never left me—the favour I ask is that it may be buried with me in my tomb, and remain for ever fastened on my heart.

With these words his strength gave way, and he sank back, grasping the memorial that was so dear to him.

At midnight on the 18th he died, and the Emperor Paul had the coolness to exclaim, on hearing of it:—

The hero has paid his tribute to Nature—his disobedience only pained me because it sullied his laurels.

Suwarow was buried with military honours, variously characterized as those of a major-general, or of a member of the Imperial family; but the courtiers saw it was not their business to attend the funeral, and the diplomatic body imitated their prudence. It is, however, to the honour of our country as well as of the individual, that the minister of Great Britain, Lord Whitworth, paid this illustrious man the homage of his respect, and saw his remains consigned to their last resting place.

When Suwarow, in passing through Moravia, visited the tomb of the brave Field-Marshal Laudohn, and read the long and pompous Latin inscription on it, he turned round and said:—

No, when I die, don't give me a long postscript like this: say only, here lies Suwarow.

And in compliance with his wish, a plain tablet of bronze bearing these words, and having a lamp above it, was erected in the church of St. Alexander Newsky; and continued, until after the death of the unfortunate Paul, the only memorial of Russia's most distinguished champion.

CHAPTER 6

On Mr. Alison's Opinion of the Archduke Charles as a Military Critic

In taking leave of (what he styles) the memoirs of the Archduke Charles, in the 5th volume of his *History of Europe*, Mr. Alison eulogises their illustrious author in these words:—

> Luminous, sagacious, disinterested, severe in judging of himself, indulgent in criticising others; liberal of praise to all but his own great achievements; profoundly skilled in the military art, and gifted with no common powers of narrative and description, his work is a model of candid and able military disquisition. On a fact stated by the archduke, whether favourable or adverse to his reputation, or a criticism made by him on others, the most perfect reliance may be placed.

I can by no means concur with Mr. Alison in regarding the archduke as "disinterested:" at least in so much of his literary labour as has reference to the campaign of 1799; as I think it easy to trace an attempt, in his relation of that period, to palliate to his contemporaries and posterity the absence of those qualities in himself as a leader of armies, which tended so materially to nullify the talents and bravery he unquestionably possessed; and which, excluding him from the grandest scenes of European glory, reduced him in 1813, to employ his leisure as a strategical casuist, in place of shining as the commanding genius of that eventful military period.

And thinking, as I do, that any one forming his opinion of the archduke from this eulogy of Mr. Alison's, and then proceeding to form his opinion of Suwarow by what the archduke has written of him, would come to very erroneous conclusions respecting the Russian hero; I desire to substantiate here the simple and altogether in-controvertible fact, that, as regards Suwarow, His Highness is neither "indulgent in criticising," nor "liberal of praise:" and further (putting liberality and indulgence out of the question), to cite one or two im-portant instances, wherein I think the criticisms he has deliberately laid before the public, so long after the events they canvass, are by no means deserving of "the perfect reliance" which Mr. Alison enjoins us to place on them.

The extent to which the archduke is "liberal of praise" towards Suwarow, may be first disposed of; as the sentence, "Suwarow's prompt and determined resolution to march from the Upper Po towards the Trebbia decided for the moment the fate of Upper Italy," constitutes the "first—the last—the only" passage of the "campaign of 1799," im-plying in any manner the approval of its author of any one of his Rus-sian co-adjutor's proceedings. And as on the march to the Trebbia is expended all the praise the archduke can afford to Suwarow, so on his comment on the succeeding battle rests the whole claim he may have, in Suwarow's case, to the epithet "indulgent" in criticising; His High-ness having therein considerately adduced an excuse for Suwarow's clumsy way of doing his work, which no other human being had ever thought of, or, indeed, considered requisite.

The "indulgent" criticism on the Battle of the Trebbia runs thus:—

Attacks repeated separately by the different arms composing the two lines, without connection—without art—without any ob-ject but that of killing each other, cost much blood, and led to no other result at the end of the second day but the greatest dis-order and the disorganisation of both armies The battle itself—which was nothing but a general *mêlée*, without plan and without manoeuvres—may find its excuse in the difficulty of handling troops on such broken ground; and probably Suwarow preferred opposing the enemy with a strong line equal to his own to risk-ing any movements before him with his Russians, who, though very brave, could not manoeuvre like the Frenchmen.

To those who have read how the French were formed at a right angle to the Po, on which their right rested; and that Suwarow's order of attack for both days was in direct *échellon* from his right—thus to throw the enemy on the river and from his expected support, at the same time threatening his line of direct retreat; and that, moreover, on the first day, this able design was successfully carried out by the Russian portion of the army, which advanced to and passed the night at Settimo, in rear of the original French position,—it must be hard to conceive how "indulgent" criticism can characterize this battle as a "general *mêlée*, without plan," and conjecture an excuse for its being so, as little borne out by the events of the battle (in which the Russian troops manoeuvred extensively and well) as is the depreciatory assumption it affects to palliate. It is also strange to have perused Mr. Alison's description of the battle, including "Suwarow's judicious plan of attack—the immense advantages of the position," won by the Russian right, &c., with the crowning eulogium on it, "as one of the most splendid feats which the history of war affords," and then to find it is with him one must canvass the archduke's claims to the epithets of "liberal of praise, and indulgent in criticising."

Having thus exhausted the instances in which the archduke's criticisms on Suwarow can by any interpretation be deemed to incline to the liberal or indulgent, I would now show, that, putting out of consideration the quality or degree of his censures on the acknowledged errors of Suwarow—as the procrastinated advance on Turin, the want of ensemble in the attacks on Novi, and the choice of the St. Gothard route to Switzerland—there is a querulous, ungenerous, disparaging, and unjust tone prominently apparent throughout the general tenor of his comments on Suwarow; of which a brief summary of the passages and silences on which this view is founded, may enable the reader to judge.

The archduke's first mention of Suwarow as taking the command of his army at Valeggio, is accompanied by a remark, that "here several days were lost in regulating the new order of things," while the date of Suwarow's arrival (the 17th April) is omitted, for it would have contradicted the assertion; as the context goes on to state, that the united Austrians and Russians advanced on the 19th to the Chiesa. The French historian, Dumas, represents, on the contrary, that Suwarow arrived in the centre of Lombardy "more rapidly than anyone could have thought it possible"; and we know that he entered Milan on the tenth day after the junction of the Russians with the Austrians at Valeggio.

On the passage of the Adda, successful in all and each of its various and difficult details—including the surprise of posts, the fixing a pontoon bridge at a point supposed too difficult to justify the attempt, and that held by the enemy; as well as the direct attacks, piercing and separating the French line into isolated portions, and involving the capture of one of its strongest divisions, and the loss of a third of its force; and the admirable nature and completeness of which, as a military operation, Dumas aptly illustrates, by contrasting it with the entire and signal failure of a similar attempt, made at precisely the same points, by the great Prince Eugene—on this noble feat of arms, the Archduke Charles can afford no single word of comment, either liberal or indulgent!

Tschubarof's or Rosenberg's affair at Basignano, the archduke represents as Suwarow's deliberate act; writing, that "he ordered the Russians to pass the Po," &c., whereas His Highness knew full well that the Russians had been ordered to pass the Po because the enemy were said to have quitted it, and that Suwarow had despatched positive orders to forbid the movement.

The archduke's opinions on the action of the Trebbia have been given, but we cannot rightly estimate the tone of his criticism on Suwarow as a general, without noticing that he is altogether silent on the most serious diminution of the means on which he calculated, through General Kray's declining to join him with his army, and by the idle squandering of the forces under Klenau and Hohenzollern, previous to his arrival. In like manner, when the archduke repeatedly represents that Suwarow undertook too many sieges, and scattered his forces too widely, in no one instance does he in the slightest degree allude to the indignant remonstrances of the brave old man against the self-seeking politicians of Vienna, who insisted on these measures; and it was not from the "indulgent" archduke's pages that Mr. Alison quoted the bitter language of an officer of the Russian staff:—

> The cursed cabinet of Vienna seeks only to retard our advance. It insists that our great Suwarow shall divide his army, and direct it at once to several points. It is to waste its time and strength in the siege of fortresses, which would fall of themselves if the French Army was destroyed.

After describing the descent of Joubert's army on Novi, the archduke remarks:—

> Suwarow remained a quiet spectator of all these movements— allowed the enemy to pass the mountains; concentrate his forces and take up a strong position, without offering him the slightest opposition; the allied advance everywhere falling back. Up to the 13th it was determined to receive the enemy on the plain. All at once the marshal changed his mind, and ordered the at-

tack upon him with 4,500 men, leaving 18,000 idle at Spinetti, Tortona, and Vighizzolo.

These insinuations are easily met by the simple statement that, Joubert's intention being to relieve the citadel of Tortona, then besieged by the Allies, Suwarow, as explained in his orders and despatches, desired to fight him on the plain between that city and Novi, where his numerous cavalry would tell; which one would have supposed, accordant to the archduke's axiom, that "in action, commanding ground gives a decisive advantage:" such advantage would have been needlessly given to Joubert, had Suwarow foolishly walked up the hills to encounter him. Suwarow's change of purpose turned altogether on that of his enemy; who (finding that, contrary to his expectation, Kray's force had joined the marshal), held fast to his position, from which he had resolved to retreat on the following day. Suwarow finding him motionless, felt that he would either fall back or entrench his position on the Novi plateau, and, therefore, at once determined to attack him. The force that remained inactive was that which watched Tortona.

The comments on Suwarow's operations in Italy wind up with a comparison between the respective doings of the marshal and Moreau, in which there is nothing objectionable or unjust, except the conjecture that "without superior means Suwarow would have probably done nothing great," followed by the cold blooded and ungenerous implication that "in Switzerland we shall see him in a different situation; forced to open the route by the St. Gothard, the advantage of superior numbers was no longer his." And what was the result of this difference in his situation, over which His Highness seems to chuckle? Did not Suwarow with his inferior means open for himself the route by the St. Gothard? Was not everything in Switzerland assigned to Suwarow, done as gloriously and successfully as men could do it?

That the general combination failed, was due to the misconduct of Korsakow, Petrarch, Jellachich, and Linken, if they were strong enough for the duties allotted to them; to the Archduke Charles or the Austrian cabinet, if they were not so. Wherever the ignominy of this failure should fall, no spot of it can touch the glory of Suwarow. The measure was ordered by the Austrian cabinet. Suwarow had no word in it but a choice between two routes. He chose the boldest, and therein he erred; but erring in his choice, he nobly made it good, and reached his goal to find all lost. Had he taken the less dangerous line, the results would have been in every respect the same; save the loss of his own gallant men, who died in this thankless cause. If this has as yet seemed doubtful to the readers of this sketch, it is hoped it may be made apparent in what follows.

Ushering in his relation of the St. Gothard march, by preliminary reflections on certain military qualities, the archduke concludes them thus:—

> Too great rashness is pardonable under certain circumstances, but slowness, irresolution, and constant change of purpose, deserve to be severely punished; for in war it is often better to adopt a defective measure than to take none, or than to choose a better one too late. The loss of time is irreparable, and nothing is so fatal as inaction.

All which, though we most potently believe, we hold it not meet to have it set down as a text to be illustrated by Suwarow's proceedings: but so, it is. And now to test its application.

On the affair at Airolo, after having stated that Schweikowski had been detached with eight battalions to turn the French position, he writes:—

> The blind courage of the Russians and the ignorance of their chief in mountain warfare, cost much blood. Suwarow knew no other way of overcoming obstacles but by open force, and all day long he was paying dearly for the slight advantages he gained: at length towards evening, Schweikowski, after having clambered over precipices and lost much time in the long circuits he had to make, appeared above the St. Gothard, and obliged the Frenchmen to retreat.

This is only remarkable as declaring that Suwarow had no way of acting but by direct attack; having previously stated that he had taken the precaution of detaching a sufficient force to turn the position, and showing eventually that it was so turned: and that only later than might have been wished, because the outflanking force had lost time. As Mr. Incledon observed, on his quotation from Holy Writ, of "a man standing on a moat, and knocking another man's eye out with a beam," "the passage is nothing—the application's everything."

The disparaging tone of the criticism is kept up by the allusion to Suwarow's "delay" at Hospital, where he arrived at midnight, and which he left at daybreak; by the mention that the Russians were encamped there "*negligemment*," they having also arrived in the dark and left it before it was light; by the objection to a non-continuance of the operations against Lecourbe beyond Seedorf, when Suwarow's prime object was to join his Austrian allies in the opposite direction; and by the unexpected presentiment before us of Suwarow "an amazed creature," as Sir Christopher Hatton says, or "*stupéfait*" as the archduke pictures him at Mutten.

The difficulties of the march to that village from Altorf, confessed-ly made manifest the error of Suwarow's choice of route. Few men would have vanquished them as he did: but still there he was, in spite of obstacles, *upon his ground*; and had his allies been there as he was, the contemplated junction would have been effected. Finding none of his promised co-operators there, and hearing of their reverses, he moved to Glaris, thirty miles to the eastward, to look for them and to enable them to join him. And here the archduke denounces him as not only flagrantly blameable himself, but, wonderful to say, as the cause of that disgraceful supineness in others, of which he complained so loudly.

Suwarow found provisions at Glaris, and halted in this new po-sition during the 2nd, 3rd, and the 4th October (his movement commenced on the 4th), undecided on the plan to be adopted. His natural rashness when obstacles were to be overcome for-sook him on this occasion, and he wavered at a time when his usual resolution might have saved him, and where nothing could be more hazardous than to halt in a defile, of which the enemy occupied all the outlets, except the paths which led to the Grisons by the valley of the higher Rhine. A rapid march from Glaris towards the lake of Wallenstadt, abandoning his stragglers and baggage animals, would have given Suwarow a better road for his retreat, and the shortest communication with the Rhine; while Rosenberg's division might have checked the enemy in the Muttenthal, as long as the operation required it. In case of a reverse, he might eventually have fallen back by Elm and the valley of the Sernst.

Rosenberg at Mutten protected Suwarow's left flank, and still kept open to him the debouche on Schwyz, in the event of any sufficient Austrian force turning up at Glaris, and enabling him to resume the offensive on that side.

On the day Suwarow left Mutten, Rosenberg was attacked there by Masséna; and again with an increased force on the 1st October. On both occasions, he signally defeated the French, pursuing them on the second day beyond Schwyz; which, by the Bräghel, is 30 long mountain miles from Glaris. Now as Rosenberg joined Suwarow on the 4th, taking into consideration the march of his troops and the time for the messenger to carry him the order to move, it seems probable that Suwarow's determination, on finding neither Austrians nor certain news of them at Glaris, must have been come to on the 2nd, the day after he arrived there.

Great as may be the archduke's authority on a point of war, I do not fear to say that for Suwarow to have marched immediately on Wallenstadt, leaving Rosenberg at Mutten, would have been probably to sacrifice—certainly to compromise—that division. No decision of Suwarow's made at Glaris could by any human possibility have brought Rosenberg there before the 3rd; on which day Gazan's and Mortier's divisions of the French Army were added to the force under Molitor, which had already, in spite of the brave Bagration's best exertions, held the main entrance to the Linth valley and the path to Wallenstadt by Mollis (and Kerenzen), against the Russians.

So that to have marched on Wallenstadt before the 4th, involved the carrying of a position which apparently baffled all they could do to win it with the sacrifice of their sick, wounded, baggage, &c.—the abandonment of Rosenberg's division in a defile of which every outlet would have been held by the enemy; and to have attempted it on that day would have required the defeat of the force which had hitherto maintained the line, reinforced by two fresh divisions.

And for what object all this desperation?—to win (with certain loss, and the abandonment of baggage, wounded, sick, and stragglers; and, moreover, a good risk of complete annihilation) a line of retreat some miles shorter than one perfectly open: for it must be borne in mind that the snow which caused the suffering of the Russians in the Sernfthal fell as they moved through it, and that the expeditious General Linken had traversed it twice without complaint a few short days before them.

Surely if Suwarow be justly blameable for choosing the hazardous and occupied line of the St. Gothard in preference to the safe and open one of the Splugen, and if, as the archduke writes, one of the two most indispensable conditions of any military operation be "the safety and the greatest security from interruption of a retreat," he must have been right in choosing that by Elm and the Sernfthal to the Rhine, rather than that by Mollis and the Kerenzen. Both are mountain paths—the one certainly better and some miles shorter than the other: but a short saving of distance and a day or two of time had now ceased to be objects; while the longer line, besides dispensing with the sacrifice of blood and the critical risks of defeat, possessed the grand advantage of saving the stragglers and the material, which moved the day before the troops, and were covered by the fighting men.

The march by Mollis would have been a repetition of Korsakow's march from Zurich—a desperate fight, whose success was to be a flight of the strong, and assured destruction or captivity to all the weak or wounded. Surely the archduke is pitifully weak in striving to give currency to this strange delusion! Nor does it seem possible (as asserted by the archduke) for a force once fairly and unsuccessfully engaged on the Kerenzen line to recover that by the Linth and Sernfthal. There are two paths from Glaris to Wallenstadt—the best by Mollis, and another by Enneda, which comes into the former by a bifurcation both at Kerenzen and Murg.

To have marched by Mollis, he must have first beaten the French Army; and then, if checked beyond it, have returned to beat them there again, before he could go back to Glaris. To have tried to evade it by taking the Enneda path, he must have quitted Glaris; which, occupied by the French, debarred all return to the Linth and Sernjthal except by again defeating them.

The criticism proceeds:—

> The supposition that the French, after their successes in the north of Switzerland, would have concentrated their chief force about the lake of Wallenstadt, was the only apparent reason which could hinder the marshal from attempting to force his way; but this reason had nothing in it (*n'etoit d'aucun poids!*)

This must strike anyone as a curious dogma, and is certainly a fire-eating style of reasoning, anything but habitual to the archduke: indeed, he is nowhere either in theory or practice, in any degree the desperado he appears in this extraordinary comment. He goes on valiantly:—

> What remains to be done, when every outlet is closed (here His Highness forgets that they were not all closed; that chosen by Suwarow being perfectly open,) but to force that one which offers most advantages; especially when the losses risked by such a resolution are not greater than those we bring on ourselves by passing in the month of October over glaciers and impracticable mountains to avoid encountering the enemy.

I dare not trust myself to characterize this paragraph. A good October is as favourable a month as any for passing the Alps (*Le mois de Septembre et plus souvent encore celui d'Octobre sont souvent les plus beaux de l'année—Ebel: 9me Section*). Linken's force had passed the mountains by Elm, while Suwarow was between Mutten and Glaris, and parties of Mortier's division passed precisely the same line, to drive the Austrians from the Col du Kimkels, on the 31st of this very October, *more than three weeks after Suwarow.* The Russians were at Matt when it began to snow; and this chance event, with the accidents it occasioned, are blazoned forth as fixed objections to a route which, but for them, need not have cost a man. Even judging thus unfairly by accidentally unfortunate results, it seems fanciful in a military critic to parallel the casualties from two stiff days march, with those that must have resulted from a mad attack upon, and a retreat through, the enemy's forces.

★★★★★★

Note:—The admirers of Suwarow, equally with his solitary depredator, have luxuriated in amplifying the difficulties of this march—the former in sympathy with, the latter in detraction of Suwarow. It was, doubtless, a rough and trying finish to this glorious struggle; but not so difficult but that the leading column and headquarters did the whole distance from Elm to Panix within the one day, 6th October. And it is a curious fact, as honourable to the Russian troops as consolatory to those who sympathize with gallant men, that these noble fellows kept so well up and together throughout the whole of this grand operation, that their total loss in killed, wounded, and missing, from first to last—from Airolo on the 24th September, to Panix on the 8th October—fighting almost every day, was less in number than that of the prisoners alone taken from General Petrasch (whose force was about half the strength of Suwarow's) in his one day's scrambling affair of the 25th September.

★★★★★★

The text goes on to say:—

We must also bear in mind that the ground below Glaris was better adapted to the Russian mode of fighting than the gorges of the valleys; and the co-operation of the Austrians, who certainly could not remain idle when they should hear of the approach of their allies, ought it not at least to have been reckoned on as something?

How could Suwarow calculate on Austrian co-operation? He was at Glaris, thirty miles on their side of the ground on which they were pledged to join him; and, though not one French soldier intervened between him and Generals Jellachich and Linken, he heard nothing from them and nothing of them, but that they had vanished. Let the archduke himself describe the nature of their co-operation even at this eleventh hour:—

> In fact Jellachich advanced to Sargans on the first report of the arrival of Suwarow in the Glaris valley, and had Wallenstadt occupied; supposing that the Russians would debouche that way. He also sent a detachment to Kerenzen, who met some troops just arrived there of Mortier's division, who fell back upon the Linth. But when Jellachich received no further intelligence he abandoned the passes by the Wallenstadt lake; and the French, on the 3rd October, took possession of Mulhorn, Kerenzen, and Murg. Petrasch, whom the archduke had repeatedly ordered to take part in Suwarow's operation, collected his troops on the 4th October between Fläsch and Maienfeld, and held himself ready to support Jellachich; but the indecision of the Russian general paralysed all these movements and produced general inactivity.

If this assertion be not a sin, then are envy, hatred, and all uncharitableness cardinal virtues! Why, these generals had been paralysed before Suwarow came into the Glaris valley. Suwarow was not to come to them upon the Rhine, but they to him, beside the Lucerne Lake or in the Linththal. Only sift this slander. The Austrians were to have combined all their means and all their efforts to facilitate and support Suwarow's march, he writes:—

> I look before everything for the junction of these troops—that once effected, I consider that the Russian troops from Italy, without a fear of check, may push on by both banks of the Lucerne Lake.

Here was he at Glaris, thirty miles to the east of the Lucerne Lake: and where were his supporters? Linken at Ilantz, Jellachich at Sargans, and Petrasch between Fläsch and Maienfeld—the three last named places, as travellers will remember, near to Ragatz, and all upon the Rhine. From these points Petrasch and Linken never moved a soldier; but Jellachich (hearing that Suwarow was at Glaris on the 2nd or 3rd of October), pushed a party to Kerenzen, but no further, because he got no news: which sounds odd, when the French and Russians were fighting at Mollis, only four English miles away. But could he not have sent an officer to look into the Glaris valley, and to have seen the Russians? For nothing earthly prevented it being done.

No! he (having heard that Suwarow was at Glaris) with his brother generals stood coolly by the Rhine, when under orders to join and support the Russians; and it is the commander who says he issued them these orders, and who details these doings, that has the conscience to print that Suwarow's indecision paralysed these *fainéans*, and produced their inactivity! Elsewhere indeed, the archduke allows that Petrasch fled too far; that Linken should not have abandoned the valley of the Linth; and that Jellachich was similarly to blame: but he would extenuate their culpability by asserting that Korsakow's retreat rendered necessary (*entraina*) that of Petrasch and those of the other generals; which is simply, and by his own showing, not the fact: Petrasch having fled to Lichtensteig on the night of the 25th, and Korsakow not having retreated till the afternoon of the following day from Zurich; to hold which was the object of his morning battle.

It is a simple matter-of-fact that had these officers halted, respectively (for *not one of them* was pursued: the few French companies that beat Jellachich having to turn from him to beat Linken, and from him to fight with Auffenberg), Petrasch at the Wildhaus, Jellachich at Kerenzen, and Linken at Schwanden, they could one and all have joined Suwarow at Glaris; and thus, by nearly doubling his force, have enabled him to hold the Linth, and, perhaps, as he had hoped, "to remedy their blunders." But the archduke shows that the chief commander, Petrasch, in his dismay, entirely lost sight of Suwarow and all consideration for him; and that, under the impulse or pretence of his false theoretical notions, he fled to secure the passes into the Vorarlberg; which, common sense would have told him, no one thought of threatening.

The archduke accuses Suwarow, to palliate the conduct of these officers; while the Emperor Paul, with greater justice, refused all further co-operation of his troops unless they were one and all brought before a military tribunal. It is for the archduke to reconcile his declaration that Suwarow's army "would have been totally destroyed, if the French, profiting by their advantages, had sent some weak detachments in pursuit of it," with the statement of his text that:—

It was closely pursued (*talonnée vivement*) as far as Matt, where it stood its ground. The French here made a fresh attack in the evening, but having failed, returned to Glaris.

Doubtless, the snow which fell here, was at least as disagreeable to the French as to the Russians.

It appears to the writer of this paper that the foregoing passages sufficiently establish his position that, as regards Suwarow, the Archduke Charles is neither "liberal of praise" nor "indulgent in criticising," and that several of his criticisms upon that leader do not deserve that "perfect reliance should be placed upon them." (See note following.)

★★★★★★

Note:—It may help to illustrate the archduke's bias in judging of his Russian co-adjutors, to give his reason for abandoning the *tête-du-pont* of Busingen, with the circumstances that led to it; set off, as the relation is, with aspersions which, be it to his credit or discredit, he never indulges in but when he speaks of Russian officers. General Korsakow's only ascertained merit was that of determined courage. At Zurich, he was everywhere in person where the fight raged hottest, and Mr. Alison justly says of the disastrous finale of the battle:—

In these desperate circumstances, Korsakow evinced a resolution as deserving of admiration as his former presumptuous conduct had been deserving of censure.

What follows will show that his misfortunes had not taken the fight out of him. Having beaten General Menard on the preceding day, Korsakow, on the 7th October, debouched, with ten battalions and twenty-two squadrons, from the works at Busingen, and advanced through the forest, uncertain what he should attempt; for his own desire not to do anything was contending in him with his just dread of responsibility in case he should do nothing to aid Suwarow. This dubious movement was therefore styled a reconnaissance. Every man who undertakes a task unwillingly, is anxious to make it as short as possible. . . . .The Russian infantry threw itself upon the enemy with such impetuosity that it drove him with considerable loss as far as Andelfingen.

Here Masséna, at the head of the grenadiers of his reserve, restored order, snatched the victory from the Russians, and forced them to fall back through the Scharen-wood, and to re-enter the works. The French remained in the wood till seven in the evening, and then attacked the fort. Two successive attacks were repulsed with great bravery. Masséna fell back upon Trüllikon, and the Russians took possession of the wood.

This looks like honest fighting at the least; but the archduke having heard of the retreat of two Russian battalions under Woinow, from Diesenhofen, and of the Austrians and Condé's corps from Constance, "afflicted at these events, and fearing that the bridge at Busingen might also be taken by the enemy," ordered Korsakow to abandon the strong *tête-du-pont* (which he had already twice so gallantly and successfully defended) and to withdraw the bridge. The untowardness of this measure is fully admitted.

The abandonment of the *tête-du-pont* at Busingen, by the Allies, was a too hasty step, as by it they deprived themselves of one great means of resuming the offensive.

And again:—

In the posture of affairs at this period, the *tête-du-pont* at Busingen might have been of great use; for the season was too advanced, and Masséna had not force sufficient to have directed any serious operation against it.

And now for "your most exquisite reason!":—

The *tête-du-pont* was abandoned because the archduke—far from distrusting the steadiness of the Russian soldiers—did not feel confident that Korsakow was seriously determined to hold it. The reiterated assurances of this general did not inspire the same trust as did the tried valour of his troops.

The archduke adds, but in no way answers the natural question, "but what motive, then, prevented the prince from putting Austrians into a work which only required 2,500 men to defend it?"

His Highness seems to have had "no sentiment." The mere picture of the unfortunate and brave Korsakow entreating and begging to be allowed to hold the post, with the dread of Suwarow's early arrival to back up his own undoubted pluck in doing so, seems enough to have touched the heart of a Rhadamanthus. But not only does the archduke make the unhappy man the scapegoat of a total loss of head on his own part, leading him to an act of which he is forced to avow the pre-eminent folly, but he does it on a plea as absolutely ridiculous and uncalled for as the measure he would palliate. I once heard a staff

officer bitterly exclaim to some surly soldiers who displeased him:—
"D— n you! you can do nothing like Christian men but fight!" but
the archduke, in his affliction, seems to have been bereft of the dis-
crimination which remained to this man in his anger.

It seems to me that Korsakow shows creditably here. His anxiety
to do something for his chief, even though ignorant of what he had to
encounter; his gallant defence of the work; his reiterated requests to be
allowed to hold it, are essentially soldierlike facts and feelings, which
no specious insinuations have a right to qualify. I cannot say I think
so much of the archduke's, nor do I much honour his highly-lauded
admission of his own errors; for many of them it would be impossible
to deny, and others are attempted to be palliated by slandering other
people. He is very far from the style of great men I admire. One of his
theoretic rules is curiously applicable to this case of Busingen. "It is a
folly to abandon an influential post before an enemy is in a condition
to take it, and merely because he may, perhaps, hereafter be enabled to
do so,"—which nobody can deny.

In speaking generally of the Russians, the archduke, after a depreciatory comment on their military qualifications and acquirements, in
which he admits they had a high reputation for courage and discipline,
concludes—"Both soldiers and officers were equally blinded by presumption." Adding:—

> This was not that noble confidence in their own means which
> elevates courage and leads to great deeds; on the contrary, it was
> an indication of a moral weakness which would lead one to
> look for a fatal dejection as the sequel of the first reverse which
> might befall them.

Now we would simply ask, what the archduke can mean by this?
If it be that this was the tone of his opinion in 1799, why, he was
mistaken; but if he means to assert at the time he wrote, that this was
then, previously or since, the temper and the failing of the Russian
Army, we fearlessly pronounce that never was there uttered a more
baseless aspersion.

Presumptuous in the archduke's eyes they may have been. Brave
men are not always as considerate in their language as they might
be. General Grumbkow, writing to Marlborough from the camp of
Charles XII. says:—

> The Swedes in general are modest, but do not scruple to de-
> clare themselves *invincible*, when the king is at their head.

It is not unlikely that the Russians of 1799, indulged in philological impertinences, as offensive to the sensitiveness they galled, as that we quote must have been to the Russians themselves, till they had nobly refuted its presumption at Pultowa. But allowing all said on this head, where are we to find authority for the consequence the archduke draws from it? When the archduke wrote, no continental army in Europe could boast a century of such unsullied and sustained blazon on its military escutcheon as that of Russia; and he who would estimate its merits highest, must examine the sequel of that misfortune which the archduke tells us was to paralyze her.

Glorious as have been the victories she has won, it is in the dread ordeal of reverse—in the stern array that checked and sobered down the buoyant courage of their enemies, stimulated by all the factitious excitement of success, after such disastrous days as those of Zorndorf, Zurich, Eylau, Friedland, Borodino, Dresden, &c.—that we see the real nobleness and soldierly distinction of the Russian Army. Where, let me ask, in its history, can be pointed out its thousands and tens of thousands surrendering without a blow, after reverse, and even before it, as has too often happened to that of Austria? When has a single battle crushed its military spirit, and prostrated its country, as that of Jena did Prussia? Or what historian can say of it, as a fellow-soldier says of that of France:—

People will naturally ask, whence it proceeds, that an army glorified by a thousand triumphs, should see panic fears so often repeated in it?

On the contrary, if there be any one characteristic of a Russian Army more essentially peculiar to it than another, as compared with its rivals in renown, it is the capability of enduring reverse without being demoralised by it. We do not, in our admiration of them, go the length of Mr. Alison, who declares, that when the iron bands of Russia came into the field, it was seen "how little all the advantages of skill and experience avail, when opposed to the indomitable courage and heroic valour of northern states!" holding that at Zurich, Austerlitz, Friedland, &c., skill and experience decidedly baffled and triumphed over all that this indomitable courage and heroic valour could oppose to them; but it certainly shakes one's confidence in Mr. Alison, to read that while such is his opinion, he bids us place reliance on all the *dicta* of the Archduke Charles.

If I am to pin my faith on this point to the opinion of an historian less partial than I may be, I confess I would give up Mr. Alison's decision for that of Capefigue, of whom Mr. Alison speaks so highly; and who, distinctly asserting that *"dans la campagne de Suwarow, l'Archiduc Charles avait pris en haine l'armée Russa,"* presents this as His Highness's reason for not having served at Austerlitz.

******

The archduke thus comments on the rage excited among the Russians by the events thus cursorily glanced over, in a dignified if not altogether dispassionate spirit.

It requires a lofty mind and a noble frankness to admit one's faults at the cost of one's self-love; and yet this is the first step towards their correction, for the conviction of our past faults must often be attended with future benefit. But ignorant and presumptuous men, possessing neither the penetration requisite to perceive their errors, nor the courage to admit them, look for the source of their failures in extraneous causes out of their control.

They commonly fix on treachery, because it is an accusation at once the easiest to make and the hardest to investigate. Thus, we see, especially in national wars, that numbers of these coarse and vulgar men always more ready than others to conceive unworthy suspicions, are particularly given to attribute their reverses to this cause. Suwarow, blinded by his victories on the shores of the Black Sea, on the Vistula, and the Po, believed himself invincible; he required a pretext to palliate his defeats. According to him. It was neither faulty dispositions in his operations, nor the errors of Korsakow that had caused them, but the treachery of the Austrians.

The opinion of the general-in-chief was taken up by the greater portion of his army, which eagerly availed itself of the means to clear itself from a fancied stain, and to preserve unsullied the glory of its arms. They affected to regard as traitors those whose cause they had defended, at the cost of too much precious blood; and thus the distrustful coldness of the Russians soon degenerated into a marked hatred of the Austrians.

Sad work this!

But och! mankind are unco weak,
And rarely to be trusted;
When self the wavering balance holds,
'Tis rarely right adjusted.

And while one regrets that Suwarow's rage at the moment should have led him to characterize the mistaken measures and inefficient co-operation of the Austrians as deliberate treachery, it excites surprise that twenty years after these events the archduke should write of Suwarow's "defeats," where he met no single check except at Mollis; and should imply that Suwarow's "faulty dispositions" had any share in the unfortunate result of the great Swiss combination, when he fulfilled in all respects every iota of that combination depending upon him.

People in England differed as to the merits of Sir John Moore's retreat on Corunna, but his bitterest asperser never dreamt of showing such extraordinary sagacity as to ascribe the defeat of the Spanish Armies, which he came to help and found annihilated, to his defective combinations. The grand error of the combination, as commanded by the Austrian Cabinet, was inherent in, and inseparable from. Itself; and this elsewhere we find in the archduke's words:—

Suwarow's movement, by whatever route he marched, had one inevitable fault, which it was out of his power to correct. The impulse and direction of the whole enterprise was to proceed from the extremity of the left wing: that is to say, from the side most distant from the true point of attack; while Masséna already possessed the advantage of having superior forces at the centre.

What rendered this error fatal, was the defeat of all the troops left to oppose these superior forces. The faults of Korsakow, mentioned by the archduke, and the faults of others not mentioned by His Highness, had much to do with this; but most of all the important fact unattended to by him, that the main body under Korsakow was left by the archduke by no means strong enough for the duty entrusted to it; and it was at once the magnitude and the apparent indefensibility of this error, that irritated the Russians to the frantic vituperation which led the archduke to pronounce them very vulgar fellows. In all the relations of mankind with each other, "exclusiveness, or the tendency to depreciate that which does not at once conform to our own taste and feelings, is a fertile source of error and of mischief;" and in recapitulating such facts as we are allowed to know of this unhappy mistake, we must bear in mind that the characters of Suwarow and the archduke were scarcely more entire antitheses to each other, than were the military opinions and methods of war of the Russian and Austrian Armies.

Their respective systems may be not unaptly characterized as the "go-a-head" and the conservative. In this campaign of 1799, the archduke's achievements showed tame and commonplace, and "paled their ineffectual fires," beside the dazzling flashes of Suwarow's glory. The latter having conquered Italy, was now apparently coming to conquer Switzerland, in which the archduke's formal modes of war had made so little progress.

The Russians are represented to us as boastful and presumptuous; and it seems as though the archduke rather sympathized, and not unnaturally, with Mrs. Quickly's disgust at swaggerers, than with Napoleon's more utilitarian feeling as regarded the boasting Poles, when he said:—

Let them boast—and woe be to them if they don't make good their words.

Certain it is that no stronger evidence is requisite than that of the archduke's book to show that he was not likely to take to the Russians kindly; and accordingly it is recorded that in less than a fortnight after they had joined him, so serious had become the want of a good understanding between him and Korsakow, that operations actually entered on were abruptly and detrimentally suspended, and the recovery of the ground by which they should have co-operated with Suwarow altogether abandoned: the archduke left Switzerland, as he relates, in utter despair of re-establishing that harmony which, we humbly think, ought to have found its best substitute in his own full power of command. He declares that, considering the state of things, "he thought it best to conform to the orders of his court, and to leave to Fate what henceforth no longer depended upon him."

This is not ferociously expressed, like the venom of some foreign ally of ours (Count Solms, I believe he was called) who in one of King William the III.'s battles, held back his help, saying, "Let's see how these English bulldogs will get out of it;" but there is certainly marvellously little in it of the genius that "rides on the whirlwind and directs the storm:" its plain English being, that, as the archduke would not conciliate, and would not command, he decided it best to follow instructions which would hold him irresponsible; though they, to his certain knowledge, seriously periled the fortunes of the whole allied cause. His anticipations of disaster are prominently made manifest, he writes:—

The prince, nevertheless, desirous that Korsakow should not be exposed to inevitable defeat (à une défaite trop certaine), and to aid him in making an honourable defence till the arrival of Suwarow, left General Hotze in Switzerland with thirty battalions and thirty-four squadrons.

He speaks of the defeat of the Russians as "too probable, look-ing to the relative weakness of their army;" and he posted the corps of Nauendorf upon the Rhine, to cover his rear, "in case the Rus-sians were obliged to give way." "The number of the Russians did not replace that of the Austrians (he again observes) between Zurich and the Rhine;" and he speaks of Suwarow's arrival as destined "to re-establish an equilibrium between the respective forces." His own conduct, he admits before he went away, exhibited "an indecision un-usual to him;" adding the sad corollary thereto, "that when the will of a commander is not decided, that of his subordinates always wavers;" and illustrating the truth by representing Hotze as becoming nervous and shaken, and adopting false measures, from apprehension of the superior force before him.

The very day before the archduke marched away from Zurich, the Austrians on the left of the army were driven entirely from the Linth; and on that very night Masséna attempted to cross the Limmat, to at-tack the united armies in all their strength, before one single Austrian soldier had moved off. Surely these demonstrations of the strength and confidence of the hostile army should have made a general-in-chief— still more "a prince of all the land" who led the war in question— pause, ere he withdrew thirty battalions and forty-two squadrons from a point thus threatened, under any considerations; trebly so under the circumstances that actually obtained. That the removal of this force to Germany at the moment was not required, is past all question. (See note following.)

★★★★★★

Note:—In truth, when in Germany, the archduke seems literally not to have known what to do with them. He says,—"The archduke, who did not attach very great importance to the fortress of Philips-burg, nor believe the corps that invested it of any great strength, had intended, on leaving Switzerland, merely to send a detachment suffi-cient to relieve that place, and to have remained himself, in the first in-stance, at the most essential point—the sources of the Danube. But be-ing soon satisfied of the weakness of the enemy on the Upper Rhine, and receiving constantly exaggerated reports of their strength on the Middle Rhine, the prince changed his mind, left 14,000 men between the Renel Valley and Waldshut, a reserve of 10,000 between Waldshut and Villengen (these independent of Nauendorf's corps of 5,400), and disposed of the remainder, so that thirty battalions and seventy-six squadrons should be collected on the 12th, between Pforzheim and

Vayhingen. As soon as the French heard of the approach of such a force, of which the cavalry spread itself on all sides, they resolved to retreat. On the 10th they abandoned Weingarten," &c.

The archduke arriving at the scene of action, and finding no enemy to fight withal, then, and then only, determined to turn his vast force upon the demi-brigade and regiment of cavalry which held Manheim, and the two battalions and as many squadrons at Neckeran, On the 18th September he captured these hosts, and then had nothing to do but to walk about the old-fashioned garden at Schwetzingen; and we hear no more of His Highness or his army till he orders Korsakow to abandon Busingen, and twenty-seven battalions, with forty-six squadrons of the force he had idly paraded about Germany during this eventful month, came back to Vayhingen between the 1st and 7th October. The misdirection of these troops formed the most palpable of the concurring causes that curiously conspired to swamp the grand Swiss combination.

To say nothing of the rest, had half the men idly posted with their left at Waldshut (ten leagues only from Zurich), while the game of life or death to the allied cause was being played in Switzerland, been added to the forces there, all might have gone well. There is, indeed, a sad probability in one of the archduke's conjectures, why the French sat down before Philipsburg, "a place altogether without influence on the operations. Perhaps," he says, "they imagined that the Austrians might relinquish more important enterprises to prevent a loss which would be a star on the glory of their arms." But if a trap was thus laid, the archduke cannot be said to have fallen—he walked—into it. So little could Philipsburg attract him, when his wishes did not point that way, that after Stockach he turned from the basin of the Danube towards Switzerland, at the very moment Bernadotte sat down before it. Philipsburg was scarcely used as a plea. The archduke was out of temper with the times, and gratified himself by doing what he liked with his own, without any very extensive consideration of how the rest of the world might be affected by it.

★★★★★★

And we cannot suppose that, if the archduke had a discretionary power to leave thirty battalions, he might not have left as many more as he deemed requisite, till Suwarow's arrival. That "the Court of Vienna commanded the secret and prompt execution of its wishes without remonstrance," is usually made the plea of all the archduke did or omitted to do at this period; but his own theory teaches us that:—

The general of an army, having the confidence of his government, should not allow himself to be discouraged by the imperfection of the plans forced upon him, and by the inconveniences they bring with them. On the contrary, it is his duty to carry them out in such a way as to prevent their disastrous consequences, and to use all his exertions to rectify their errors, though others may be answerable for them.

And indeed, looking to facts, we find him so little controlled by these orders, that, weeks after he had received them, and subsequent to the junction of Korsakow, we find him so largely a free agent as to be engaged in an operation, the effect of which, if successful, would have been to have carried his whole army so deep into the forbidden Switzerland, as to have placed it between the lakes of Neufchatel and Geneva. Of course, I allude to the passage of the Aar which was attempted on the 16th August, and failed. (See note following.)

★★★★★★

Note:—The incidents of this failure are curiously interesting and instructive to military readers. Two bridges were to have been fixed, the one above the other, below Gross Dettingen, where the river forms a bend to the east or Austrian side; the high ground of which completely commands the plain on the opposite side, on which the village of Klein Dettingen was held by two French (or rather Swiss) companies. The only French troops near the scene of the operation were 2,000 between Baden and Bernau on the Rhine; 1,500 at Laufenberg, eight miles to the west; and 600 at Lenzburg, fourteen miles to the south; while the main army was on the Uetli, more than twenty miles away.

The march of the troops to the place of assembly was so well arranged, that the different corps, concealed by the inequalities of the ground, arrived at nightfall without being perceived by the enemy, and formed in columns according to their several destinations (50,000 men with 10,000 others directly co-operating on the Rhine and Limmat, besides 8,000 in Zurich, and the forces on the Linth). The vigilance of the advanced posts prevented the enemy having the slightest suspicion of the project; but the enterprise failed through the dispositions for the passage of the river. Those charged with the fixing of the bridges had neglected to obtain the requisite knowledge of the locale, contenting themselves with simply ascertaining the breadth of the stream. They had provided boats enough for two bridges, but none to meet unforeseen contingencies.

The ground above the intended point of passage did not admit of the assembling and working of the pontoons; the steep path near Gross Dettingen rendered their descent to the river's side very difficult; the bank was not low enough; they found neither firm ground to work upon, nor easy slope to launch the boats, and direct them towards the landing-place; and as they had limited themselves to the number necessary for the bridges, there were none disposable to carry over troops. The rapidity of the current threatened to carry down the boats far below the landing-places; it would have then been necessary to drag them up against the stream, which required much time and labour, and the completion of the bridge would have been delayed.

The archduke, who, to keep the project unsuspected, had not reconnoitred the ground himself, and who only arrived on the spot during the night of the 16th, reckoned so confidently on the command of the right bank, that he expected to clear the left one by the effect of his artillery; and the work was begun without having, in the first instance, thrown over any troops to the opposite shore. The Austrians having established batteries on the heights of Gross Dettingen, commenced their work two hours after midnight. Directly the French at Klein Dettingen perceived the unusual stir, they opened a smart fire on the spot whence the noise came, and an Austrian battalion posted at Gross Dettingen, returned it in volleys of musquetry. The artillery then opened, and the village of Klein Dettingen was soon in flames.

The French, however, would not quit it, but continued to fire on their enemy; whom a thick fog concealed from them even after day broke. Notwithstanding this circumstance, so favourable to the Austrians, their work did not get on. The anchors would not hold on the rocky bottom, and they had no means of remedying this. They were not even supplied with cables to secure the boats; some of them leaked, others dragged—in a word, there was an unpardonable neglect and shameful disorder in all the preparations of this department of the army; and it was only after great exertions that, at nine o'clock in the morning, they had succeeded in making fast thirteen boats at the upper, and still fewer at the lower bridge.

The fog having then cleared away, the fire of the French became so deadly that all the pontoniers employed were successively killed or wounded. In the meantime, the artillery fire had awoke the French quartered between Bruck and Sekingen. All hurried to the direction of the fire, and Generals Ney and Hendlet assembled men enough to occupy the woods and heights which border the plain of Klein

Dettingen and the neighbourhood of Botzstein. The archduke's attempt had failed, and the cannonade, now become useless, ended by an agreement allowing the Austrians to take their pontoons from the water without hindrance.

The archduke proceeds, after detailing what should be the custom of war in like cases, to pronounce that the only reproach connected therewith which the general-in-chief has to urge against himself in similar instances of failure, is, "the men employed were not the men he took them for;" adding, that "the general of an army, occupied with great conceptions, and giving his attention to the whole vast extent of the theatre of war, cannot and ought not to enter into the petty details of the service."

Different generals take different views on this important point; but surely a general on the spot, who sanctions by his presence such procedures as the beginning to lay a pontoon bridge over a river 180 feet wide, defended by only two companies, before the pontoons had carried over 500 men to capture or disperse them, so that the work might begin from both sides at once; and, this being neglected, allows artillery to blaze away in the dark, with the mad hope of dispersing a few *tirailleurs*, and the certain effect of bringing rapidly to the spot every Frenchman within hearing, may be not illiberally suspected of having mistaken something more than the capabilities of his officers. I do not think any soldier would have believed such wondrous oversights on the part of so renowned an officer, but on his own authority.

And equally wonderful are the deficiencies of the pontoon department, for Austria had been warring incessantly (except for one year) since 1792! But when the anchors would not bite, pontoniers, army, staff, and all seemed "*au bout de leur science*," and with night and fog to aid them, with their enemy's troops placed as if to insure the success of their enterprise, the prince and his host had to retire; owing their discomfiture to two companies of infantry. The prince praises them, as he ought: but for their gallantry, he would have had no single extraneous excuse for his failure.

"Two French companies," he says, "stopped 50,000 men, and this handful of brave men deserve the highest praise. Neither the shower of balls and musquetry, which the Austrians poured upon them, nor the firing of the village, could shake their intrepidity; but, taking advantage of the cover which, the ruins of the houses gave them, they stood firm amid the conflagration.

"'Brave, by Heaven! They'll go to heaven for it, your honour,' says

Trim. 'They will,' said my Uncle Toby."

If there is one thing, I love to come upon in military history more than aught else it affords, it is these instances which show what a few steady men, under a captain or subaltern worthy of them, may do when they resolve to do their utmost. Blessed fellows, who facing a host, a hundredth part of which, rightly used, could crush them at an effort, feel "how little they can do—and yet do that." It is the poetry of duty. The actual realisation of the ideal in what is noblest in man. The artist may give us form and grace which no human archetype can match, but vainly must the poet labour who would fancy acts more lofty in their quality than those of absolute devotion to a duty.

★★★★★★

When the violation of the Vienna instructions, elsewhere regarded as so peremptory, is thus cavalierly disposed of:—

His success might have been accepted as an excuse for his not having followed to the letter the instructions he had received. Perhaps they would not have held him back or turned him aside from the object to which he was rapidly advancing; and if even they had subsequently made him leave Switzerland, and give up the scene of his exploits to the Russians, they would have owed to the archduke the expulsion of the enemy.

Seeing how little these Vienna orders hampered the archduke, in what he wished to do with the whole of his force, it is impossible to suppose they could have tied up his discretion as regards the temporary distribution of a part of it.

It was in this view, therefore, that the Russians ascribed to the archduke the sacrifice of Korsakow's force, by his unnecessary removal of so large a mass of the Austrians to Germany previous to the junction; and at the time of these events they believed that the same authority which had compromised Korsakow, must have prescribed the inexplicable conduct of the Austrian generals left to aid him; contrasting, as it did, with the zeal and gallantry of Kray, Auffenberg, and other Austrian generals who had warred by their side in Italy. Their aspersions are indefensible; but that the grounds of their complaint were solid and just, is thus admitted by the archduke:—

An impartial judge, looking at the circumstances without prejudice, and considering only the course most fitted to have attained great ends, will reproach the archduke for having preferred the relief of Philipsburg to a more important object; for having left Switzerland before the arrival of Suwarow, or, at any rate, before serious danger threatened his communications in the valley of the Danube; for not having remained personally in Switzerland, so as to reconcile and regulate, by his authority, the peculiar views of Hotze and Korsakow; and for not having left there as many troops as would have equalled the enemy's forces: especially as the operations of the French were not so serious as to require more than 40,000 men to be opposed to them. This, however, one could scarcely know at the moment.

A less severe observer will see in the embarrassing position of the archduke, and in his faults, a new proof of the dangers incurred when Cabinets, far from the theatre of events, give, during the course of a campaign, precise orders on the direction of operations, instead of pointing out to their commanders general views by which they are to be guided. But this same observer cannot refrain from blaming the archduke's indecision, when, sending Hotze to Rapperschwyl on the 17th August, he did not by a determined will, and by positive orders, oblige the Austrian and Russian generals to proceed with vigour, and without reply, in carrying out the operations to the left of the lake of Zurich; which it is possible might have re-established matters.

This candid admission, seen by itself, would silence further depreciatory comment on the archduke; but, coming as it does after so much said and implied to decry Suwarow, and to throw on him the blame of this very failure, it rather disturbs than disarms the feeling previously excited.

Advocating the conviction that Suwarow, with all his oddities, affords a grand example of the power of that earnestness and devotion, inherent and capable of beneficial development in large masses of the great human family, we find additional satisfaction in this belief from the opportunity now afforded of contrasting, not so much his sayings (though these may well bear scrutiny) as his doings—his decision and energy communicated to all around him, his untiring self-employment, his aid to operations undertaken in opposition to his views, his cordial conciliation or efficient command of the allied troops employed under him, his whole conduct as a chief of armies, in short—with the parallel proceedings of the accomplished general, who, in his writings, exerts the cultivated powers of his mind and the influence of his position to dim a great contemporary's reputation.

Suwarow may, in the opinion of many, have deserved the epithets of "coarse and vulgar;" but superior qualities for national service, unacknowledged in this archduke's work, are as unquestionably the just attributes of Suwarow, as are the strongly developed military deficiencies and personal weaknesses made manifest in it—the failings of the Archduke Charles; who brought the jealous and nervous sensibilities of a court-bred prince into the rugged game of war (where the sterling qualities of Nature's noblemen alone make weight) as well as to his labours as an author, in which their unwholesome bias has led to omissions and palliative relations amounting to constructive falsehood; and he really looks little, with all his theory and acquirements, beside the rough old hero, who dwarfed him by his propinquity.

If he did not feel and writhe under the consciousness of this, from first to last, in 1799, the tone of his work has very much misled me. Whatever be the cause, the Vienna booksellers declare the book to be now (1846) completely out of favour with His Highness, who would gladly circumscribe its further circulation. But it has unfortunately become history, and the archduke's better after-thought (like many others apparently in his eventful life) has come too late.

It seems to me that writers on military science are too apt (unconsciously perhaps) to glide into the currier's error of "nothing like leather;" and in their appreciation of the science they inculcate, to tend by their doctrine to cramp and depreciate the glorious qualities of military energy and daring: much as the engineers of the olden time were accustomed to do by their continuous lines of fortification, which often gave a weak support, while they paralyzed the action which, but for their restraint, might have led to victory.

The tone and tenor of the Archduke Charles's work on the campaign of 1799, renders it, in my humble opinion, largely amenable to this impeachment, when shewing, as it does in an able (though I think uncandid) military disquisition, what Moreau and Napoleon had already sufficiently and practically proved, *viz.*, that the valley of the Danube was the true line of attack on Austria: it exhibits its author so engrossingly impressed with the importance of the adoption of a true line of military operation, as to allow himself to be misled, in its exemplification, to an apparent underestimate of a still more important essential in war, *viz.*, that moral force, without which the strategic talent of a commander becomes inefficient and resultless.

If the game of war were played like that of chess, we doubt not the archduke's theory would teach a man to checkmate his adversary, provided always he were allowed to be as long about it as suited his convenience; but unluckily for skill, the rough players at war are allowed to sweep the table and seize the stakes if they can; and there is nothing in its rules to secure a general, who shall be as careful as the archduke would have him to keep the key of the theatre of war in his hands, from seeing the door kicked open in spite of him, and the said theatre in the hands of his antagonist. General Mack in 1805, and the archduke in 1809, were in possession of the key; but "they couldna haud it."

Paradoxical as it may seem, I think it dangerous to illustrate the principles of strategy by a detailed history of a period of actual war. To judge of the strategical correctness of a given operation by testing its application to established axioms, is a sound and instructive process, by which you will see whether it was or was not according to strategic rule; but to relate the operations of a campaign, applying to each and all of them strategic principles as gauges of their excellence, would in many cases be as childish a procedure, as to bring forward the pace stick and plummet of the drill sergeant, as the standards by which you must condemn the lengthened strides and rapid dash with which devotedness would rush to victory.

The science of strategy is matter of demonstration, and its best illustration is a diagram. Its deductions are invariable and immutable as regards a given theatre of war, whose lines of least resistance will always be the same, whatever may be the various qualities of the armies or the personal attributes of the commanders engaged in it. Strategic science is to the game of war what "Matthews" is to the game of whist; but, unfortunately for the science, the pre-established value of the cards in hand. In the game of war, alters as the game goes on; and when the ten will no longer beat the nine, results become necessarily uncertain. The archduke admits this fully.

The majority of all the powers which constitute the material force of armies, does not in all cases ensure success in war to him who wields them. An antagonist who knows the art of employing them, and giving to them a more forcible action, will often vanquish it. Herein lies the secret of moral force; and as in war this moral force, whether exhibited by a commander or his troops, constitutes a power that very commonly baffles calculation, the chief who knows he wields it is often justified and to be lauded for disregarding rules and precautions, which prudence and science would alike wisely prescribe, where that equality existed on which must rest the deductions of demonstrative science.

But the object of a writer on military strategy being to show that the principles of the science are truths, and to inculcate an adherence to them, in doing this, seldom gives due consideration or weight to those circumstances which, changing the value of the premises or data of a problem, render these rules inapplicable to it. Such circumstances find little favour in his sight—they seem to him impertinent anomalies: he is apt to under-estimate their weight, and not unfrequently to give them ugly epithets. And thus we find the value of moral force, which no man had better opportunities of estimating than the Archduke Charles, though admitted as a power in war, so often questioned for its successes, and so believed for its excesses; and those possessing most of it so little applauded for it, that the impression left on the mind is, that in the archduke's opinion it is a very doubtful and dangerous quality to depend on.

Now, this in a military history, seems the most detrimental of all possible biases; and, as I think, most peculiarly so in a history addressed to the Austrian Army: whose defects, as depicted even by the archduke himself, seem those especially originating in a want of the very quality he gives the weight of his authority to depreciate. Not but that the archduke fully admits that "a decided resolution is in general the first quality of the soldier, and the distinguished characteristic of his calling," but this cold assertion of a truth is far from the impressive enforcements of it which his subject called for.

It is in shewing where this first of qualities has been most gloriously exhibited, and where it has been proved to have been most palpably wanting, that men are made to feel its value, and to receive into their minds impressions that may influence their future character. Acknowledging a power in moral force, the archduke damns it with faint praise; and admitting its success, laboriously points out where its proceedings were theoretically wrong, without emphatically shewing how much more so was the want of energy that caused it to be successful.

By way of instance, His Highness shews at length how Lecourbe sinned against rule in his glorious advance on Zernetz; and then concludes:—

Lecourbe allowed himself to be carried away by his intrepidity and the violence of his character; preferring to force his way, and not caring for the blood of his soldiers when he thought the shedding; it would give him success, he trusted blindly to the superiority derivable from acting on the offensive, and taking the initiative in his operations: and indeed, nowhere are such means more decisive than in mountain warfare.

Surely in this Lecourbe was right. He knew and felt the power of moral force; he wielded and used it to success. But it would have been folly to have lost time or opportunity in acting by rule, or not acting at all, when the quality of the opposition he anticipated could be braved as he braved it. The glaring deficiency prominent in this operation, was the want of moral force on the Austrian side. On this Lecourbe calculated, and calculated rightly. He did not think his antagonists had it in them to break in on his long line, down the Inn, by the difficult lateral valleys that gave access to it: but the thing was possible, and, therefore, the strategical teacher has a right to shake his head at him. Again, when Dessolles succeeds at Taufers against more than twice his force of Austrians, the archduke's comment simply acquaints us that:—

He dared not have done as he did, had he had an enterprising enemy before him; and that nothing but the disposition of the ground, the well-known character of an antagonist, and of his mode of acting in war, could justify expeditions of the kind.

Granted fully: but as these all did justify the case in point, what more was requisite?

And here let it not be supposed I idly cavil at the archduke: his strategical arguments are amply borne out by the subsequent nullification of the effects of these brilliant successes, through the results of operations in other quarters; and he is, of course, in every respect right to show in how much certain operations were hazardous: but what seems to me deficient in his teaching, is the absence it exhibits of all due appreciation, stimulation, and upholding to highest honour and emulation, of that executive energy and daring, which gave success to measures that, theoretically speaking, did not deserve it.

No soldier who knows his business can undervalue the great influence of science or of methods of war: where moral force and numbers are equal, these insure success; but no science, nor any methods of war, can in the long run compensate for a great inferiority of moral force; and it is a source of mystification and error so to illustrate the advantages of these, as to set aside the prominent advocacy and inculcation of the higher and more important truth, on a due understanding and appreciation of which the security and honour of nations can alone be based with confidence.

Long after Attila had scoffed at "the degenerate Romans, whose deep and compact order of battle betrayed their fears," we find in the tactics of Leo and Constantine Porphyrogenitus a return to a sounder system of formation, approaching closely to that which Gustavus Adolphus subsequently adopted: but it was all in vain, because, as the historian remarks:—

Neither authority nor art could frame the important constituents of these formations—the soldier!

Nor justly can it be urged that, because the archduke's work is most professedly a scientific one, we are, therefore, solely to look to it for scientific teaching. Had the purport of the work been thus exclusive, my objections to it would not have been excited. But while judging of events by their concordance with, or disregard of, the principles of science, His Highness has spoken exclusively of moral force; though always coldly, and often depreciatingly. Of all the French generals, he most frequently blames Lecourbe, at once the boldest and most successful of them. We have seen how little praise he can afford to the matchless daring and perseverance of Suwarow. He cannot deny the superior bravery of the Russian troops, but he detracts from it by insinuations.

And so far, does His Highness carry this tendency to throw the drawback of his indifference over success obtained by moral force, that he systematically avoids any distinct or distinguishing comment on those feats of his own officers which are glorified by the quality he delights not to honour. Auffenberg, at Amsteg; Major Etwas, at Schwyz; and Klenau, near Genoa, showed an energy in difficulties that ennobles them in the eyes of others; but they find no eulogist in their unimpassioned chief. He says, speaking of the constituents of moral force:—

Springs of action of that temper sometimes even balance a superiority of numbers, but they cannot hold out against it, because will alone is powerless when means are wanting to it.

Why, so is science, and so is all else in war; but moral force will often triumph over numbers and science, whereas mere science, or numbers without it, is the veriest broken reed that ever calculators leant on. Again he writes:—

Small armies possessed of great moral force have vanquished colossal masses, whilst hordes of barbarians have beaten the best disciplined armies on earth, by the mere superiority of their physical powers.

To which latter phrase we demur to subscribe, believing that without a superiority of moral force in the said barbarians, this latter contingency would never happen. The mobs of Russians that baffled all Frederick's science at Künersdorf, and the Circassians who now annually baffle their descendants, do not do this, as it appears to me, by superior physical strength, but by the superiority of their moral force. They hold on longer and steadier to the simple and sublime motto, "*malo mori quam fudari*," than their antagonists. And to do this is the first and grandest of all military qualities, and should be upheld by every military teacher as such.

A demonstration that success obtained by moral force in disregard of strategical principles is wrong, as tested by the principles that are true and immutable, and only defensible as a lucky result worked out by a power always accidental, assuredly leads to the conclusion, that as a man may be wrong in his conjectures of the degree of moral force he wields, he would be safest and wisest in guiding himself by the principles which are sound in themselves and eternal in their application; and this, we think, must inevitably lead, in minds of dubious temper, to the adoption of vague ideas of a supposed knowledge, which may too often prove their excuse for choosing a safe rather than a perilous alternative—as, for instance in the case of Petrasch when he fled from the support of Suwarow, because he was so learned in strategy as to suppose the fate of Austria rested on his occupation of the Vorarlberg passes.

No army in Europe has suffered so much from blots of this nature as that of Austria, and we fear the archduke's teaching has no tendency to diminish them. A military history should inculcate, with a trumpet's tone, those qualities that constitute the highest power of armies; and he who so advocates any of the accessory helps in war, as to leave it dubious whether an adherence to them may not be more incumbent on the soldier than his adhesion to this first great duty, will do an injury to the cause he advocates which all the theory he may teach will never remedy. History is philosophy teaching by example. Alexander slept with Homer under his pillow. What English soldier does not feel convinced, on reading Napier's history or Mitchell's essays, that he could have done the deeds they narrate, and would be ready to do them if called upon?

But who could by any possibility imagine a man animated to any nobler course than his self-seeking instincts would suggest, by any excitement he would owe to a history such as that of the archduke?

What has been wanting in the Austrian Army, for which the arch-duke writes, is energy. Their system based on ideal knowledge of war, which over-estimating its material and scientific agencies has over-looked what may be done by energy and devotedness, has given to their operations so conservative a character,—such a habit of looking backward rather than onward, and a promptness to abandon all effort the moment that chances seem to preponderate against them—as often to paralyze, and almost always to impair, their power as an army. See what Napoleon says of the Austrians—

No people on earth are less active or dangerous as regards military affairs than they are.

What is his most contemptuous censure of soldiers of his own:—

Les misérables! Ils se laissent battre même par des Autrichiens.

Foy declares:—

It was sufficient for the acquittal of their conscience that the wings were turned, or merely passed; their battalions, drawn up so laboriously in right lines, immediately took to their heels. Our foot soldiers of three feet high brought in the giants of Germany and Croatia by hundreds.

In the archduke's pages we read of "their slowness, which could never avail itself of advantages, though backed by numerical superiority;" "their exaggerated fear of being turned, which terrified them, and often led to the greatest calamities;" and in the following passage we have a picture in little of all we would have understood on this particular point:—

During our latter wars, the incapacity of commanders on either side has produced effects on the German and the French diametrically opposite to each other. It made the former hesitating—the latter rash. The French, excited by revolutionary enthusiasm, sought to trample on obstacles, and when they saw a danger to brave, sought for victory as the result: this was the impulse they followed when they had no more certain guide. The Germans, trained to passive subordination, slaves of discipline and fixed rules, restrained by responsibilities, fell into the paralysis of irresolution when circumstances became embarrassing.

Surely, to such an army, a work of the temper of the archduke's is

171

a fatal legacy!

Inculcate true principles of strategy among them, in the name of Heaven I but do not let it be so done as to blind them to what is a thousand times more requisite to them as an army. The great and palpable defect of the Austrian Army, when the archduke wrote, was want of energy in those who led them. When the French officers had to speak of one of them who was bold and daring, it was as an exception to the rule:—

Il navait rien du caractère méticuleux des Autrichiens; il était, comme on dit, franc du collier, ses attaques étoient poussées au fond.

To an army of this character, a work like the archduke's is rather calculated to perpetuate its formal mediocrity than to elevate its tone and lend glory to its future. Give every man in it all the science the archduke ever had, with the deficiencies of energy and decision that were associated with it, and they would be no whit more capable of warring with the French, on an equal footing, than they have been. Teaching such as the archduke's, is like the generalship that mistakes or prefers a secondary to a primary object—its success even may be nullified by the influence of what it has disregarded. An army without high tone and energy is like a locomotive bereft or short of steam.

The engine under its full impulsive power may occasionally run off the line—blow up or come to other mischief; but without it, or with a supply that only works it inefficiently, its "being's end and aim" are nullified, and it stands a great combination of artificial construction and admirable skill, got up at an enormous expense, to tantalise and provoke those interested in it by its failures and shortcomings. See the picture the archduke gives us of the commonplace man in action:—

Seldom does the same man conjoin such perspicacity in his views and firmness in his resolutions, that, at the decisive moment, he will not be shaken by doubt; even should no indirect motive of his own suggest them.

Take a single instance, out of the thousand parallel cases the history of the Austrian Army furnishes, of an officer believing that, according to his military ideas, it was time for him to surrender, from St. Cyr's account of the affair of Castelfranco:—

Nous avions à peine assez d'hommes pour se saiser des chevaux montés par la cavalerie ennemie. Le vieil officier qui commandait le regiment de Cuirassiers de l'Archiduc Ferdinand remit son epée, les larmes aux

yeux, et non sans beaucoup d'hésitation. 'Je crois, Monsieur le Général,'
disoit il, 'je crois que vous n'êtes pas fort.'

What this poor old fellow wanted was something sure—something borne in upon his mind like the Moslem impulse, "Paradise is before you—hell and the devil in your rear,"—something by which he should know that it was good to fight till he could fight no longer; and surely to the army, of which very probably he was a very worthy member, it cannot be good for their greatest chief to shew no sympathetic thrill while detailing gallant deeds—to studiously refrain from eulogy where brave men rise above the average of their fellows, as well as from branding the shameless, and almost palliating pusillanimity and fatuity by the faintness of his objections to them.

Jomini in his scientific treatise on great military operations does not do this; but he, too, affords an evidence of the difficulty to the human mind of justly judging of all the various points of war, when strongly biased by those scientific formula, whose general application must rest on the assumption that men, like similar lines in a demonstration, are equal quantities. With the staring fact before him of the superiority of his own fellow-soldiers in moral force to many of the armies they had to contend with, he is driven, in the illustration of his universal principles, to assume that all warring civilized nations are so nearly equal in warlike attributes, that similar formations must be advisable under similar circumstances alike for all peoples; and in recommending his columns of attack for actual battle, he dismisses the result of the ten campaigns in which the English have invariably beaten these columns by their lines, with the foolish sneer that it was the fault of those who allowed themselves to be beaten by such a method of war that they did so. Whereas nothing can be more palpable, that to fight in line against columns gives more fire—suffers less loss from hostile projectiles—and, above all, affords a powerful disposable reserve (on which he admits that success mainly depends) wherever numbers are equal.

A hundred years ago. Marshal Saxe told the French infantry that they were not adequate to act in line on open ground against a brave enemy who did not fear to charge; and though we do not know why he thought so, we know that facts have borne him out in his opinion. And therein we see the justification of their adoption of the barbarous and blood-wasting action by columns, in a time of war when greatest damage is done by forcible and far-reaching projectiles. But surely this is no reason for its adoption by those who can dispense with so extravagant and irrational a formation.

Looking, then, to the cause of this delusion on the part of Jomini, we can alone ascribe it to that natural bias in favour of his own gallant brother-soldiers which would not allow him to acknowledge any inferiority in them, such as could only be accounted for by admitting a superiority in others. In like manner, we believe the Archduke Charles is led to screen the deficiencies of the army he loved, by shirking and mystifying the effects of the qualities in which they are apparently deficient, and dwelling as of most importance on the secondary talent in which he, if not they, may be pronounced superior.

In this mistaken preference of so high an authority in the Austrian Army, we imagine we see some elucidation of the otherwise unaccountable fact, that, with perhaps the most variably adapted military population on earth—strong in numbers and goodwill—Austria has never, during the course of modern history, carried to a successful termination any war in which she has combated single-handed; nor has ever allied herself with other powers without having excited an universal and detrimental impression of her slowness and want of energy.

Il faut que le général ne donne pas mains de soin au moral de son armèe. A quoi servirait en effet que cinquante mille hommes fussent mis en bataille devant vingt mille, s'ils manquent de l'impulsion nécéssaire pour enlever et culbuter l'ennemi? Ce nest pas seulement du soldat dont il s'agit, c'est plus particulièrement encore de ceux qui doivent le condnire—is the crowning teaching of Jomini's admirable scientific treatise.

The gallant Foy, with the painful but honourable justice towards those who crushed the cause he served says:—

Yes, doubtless, doubtless the instinctive determination which even when it errs is better than skilful hesitation—the strength of mind that no danger can appal—the tenacity which carries off the prey by sticking to it to the last—these are rare and sublime qualities.

And these rare and sublime qualities, as it appears to me, are either not regarded as such by the Archduke Charles (judging from the text and tone of his campaign of 1799), or he has been betrayed into refraining from their prominent inculcation, either by the consciousness that they were by no means brilliantly exhibited by himself or his army during that period, or by a protracted and rankling estrangement

from the Russian Army, whose conduct formed so noble and incessant a display of them. If the first, would it not rather militate against
him as a chief of armies—if the second, as an indulgent and liberal
military-writer to whose statements and opinions implicit reliance
must be given? His work I think an able disquisition on strategy, but
a military history deficient in important essentials; and most especially
ill-adapted to improve the army for whose particular instruction it
was written.

CHAPTER 7

A Few Objections to Certain Military Statements and Opinions in Mr. Alison's History

Having thus endeavoured to throw my feather weight into the scale against the assumed liberality and infallibility of the archduke's judgment as regards Suwarow, I think it right, before laying down my pen, to notice a few points of Mr. Alison's relation of the events of 1799, wherein I presume to think he has written without due care and consideration. I have read no more of his work than the narration of the events of that period; and though I have found in what I have perused many large views of strategy, military parallels, and causes and effects, from which I heartily and entirely dissent, I shall leave untouched these more intellectual topics, and restrict my observations to such simpler matters-of-fact as it may not seem presumptuous in me to canvass.

Most men think unfavourably of the Archduke Charles's generalship, when, after gaining the Battle of Stockach, he allowed Jourdan's beaten and divided army to retire unmolested. Monsieur Thiers says:—

> The Austrians, exhausted by this long battle, dared not pursue us. If the archduke, profiting by his advantages, had actively followed the beaten army, he might have thrown it into complete disorder, and perhaps even destroyed it.

Marshal Gouvion St. Cyr (who commanded a division at Stockach) remarks:—

> Nevertheless, the archduke did not profit by the advantage this

event had given him; he was afraid to follow the force he had beaten, and stopped the movement of his army.

It would be interesting to know the cause of this, and it was looked for from the frankness of his character in the work he has published; but there we only find, that:—

Satisfied with having decided the victory, the prince did not advance into the plain. When a general believes he has gained a victory, it is his business to profit by it.

Mr. Alison, more condescending than the archduke, thus explains in his sixth volume, the reason of His Highness's inaction:—

With superior forces and 20,000 cavalry in admirable order, the Austrians had now an opportunity of overwhelming the French Army in the course of its retreat to the Rhine, such as never again occurred to thein till the Battle of Leipzic. The archduke clearly perceived that there was the important point of the campaign; and had he been the unfettered master of his actions he would in all probability have constrained the enemy's army to a retreat as disastrous as that from Wurtzburg in 1796. But the Aulic Council forbade him to advance towards the Rhine till Switzerland was cleared of the enemy. He was compelled, in consequence, to put his army into cantonment between Engen and Wahlwies, while the Republicans leisurely effected their retreat through the Black Forest.

Here Mr. Alison pronounces that the instructions of the Aulic Council as to operations on the Rhine compelled the archduke to put his army into cantonment after Stockach, and thus to allow the Republicans to retreat leisurely; whereas the truth is, that the archduke, gaining the battle on the 25th of March, did not put his army into cantonment till the 6th April, when the retreat of the Republicans was completed.

It is for his supineness during the intermediate period that men hold him faulty, and ask his reasons. The Aulic Council had ordered him to advance from the Lech to meet the French near the sources of the Danube. He met them, fought them, and beat them; separating their force so completely, that while one portion retreated to the west, the other retreated to the north, and only effected its reunion with the main army by forced marches, on the third night after the battle. Friends and foes alike ask why did not the archduke profit by this opportunity of destroying one or other of these bodies; and Mr. Alison acquaints us that, by some preposterous ingenuity, it was discovered that the orders of the Aulic Council regarding operations on the Rhine forbade it.

But the archduke by no means supports him in this extraordinary view. His Highness's relation shows palpably, and in spite of mere verbiage, that what was wanting in him on this occasion was that energy and decision which the Aulic Council had as little power to take from as to give him. In Suwarow's words, "He didn't *half* will!"

St. Cyr's quotation, that, "satisfied with having decided the victory, the prince did not advance into the plain," shows him, on the battlefield, a general of the class of Sir Harry Burrard at Vimiera; and the following day (the 26th) we read, that:

> Looking at Switzerland as the point of most importance, and strongly persuaded that Jourdan would not halt on this side of the Black Forest, he thought it sufficient to follow him with a mere advanced guard.

But, lo! Jourdan did halt on this side of the Black Forest, and then (on the 28th) the archduke determined "to suspend everything, till he should have driven him into the valley of the Rhine;" and on the 29th and 30th he was reconcentrating his army on the Stockach ground, and uniting it to Sztarray's corps for this purpose. With these forces he was at Donauschingen on the 3rd April, and beyond this entrusted the pursuit to Sztarray.

It is these shilly-shally proceedings, with a glorious opportunity before him, which derogate from the archduke's character as a general; and nothing but mystification or delusion can seek to represent them as any way affected by the subsequent cantoning of the army on the 6th April. To coincide with Mr. Alison's view, we must suppose the archduke fettered by the Aulic paralysis on the 25th, 26th, 27th, and 28th March, and forced from it on the 29th, 30th, and 31st, and that the French Army owed its safety on all these days to the cantoning of the army on the 6th of the following month. It is possible that Mr. Alison may have been misled by a paragraph in the archduke's work, inserted (rather Jesuitically as it seems) between the relation of the events of the 27th and 29th March. It runs:—

> At this epoch unfortunate events checked the progress of operations. The archduke was attacked with sudden illness—the court of Vienna was disinclined to successes which should appear

to expose the Tyrol, by removing the army from the supposed theatre of war. These contrarieties paralyzed the activity of the archduke, and favoured the retreat of the French. The Austrians neglected the opportunity of falling on the divided forces of the enemy, putting him out of condition to hold the field, &c.

But a military critic should have borne in mind that it was on the 26th and 27th of March, while the French Army was divided and demoralised by its defeat, that the archduke had the game in his hands; and that the feelings of the Vienna Cabinet in no way prevented His Highness subsequently following the French Army leisurely, and lukewarmly doing them no injury, just as far as a vigorous pursuit of them at the proper moment would have led him. Nor did the illness of the archduke occur so as to prevent his pursuit of Jourdan; but nearly a fortnight subsequent to the arrival of that general's army in France. It is this fact, and the too comprehensive term of epoch used by the archduke, which gives a character of deceit to the passage introduced in his context.

In fine, I meet Mr. Alison's declaration with the observation, that the Republicans did not effect their retreat leisurely because the archduke cantoned his army on the 6th April, but because he did not use his army energetically before he so cantoned it; as, on the day he did so, they had actually crossed the Rhine. I deny that the Aulic Council prevented a pursuit of the French; for the French were pursued, and only escaped severe loss because they were pursued (in the archduke's own words) "*faiblement*," which prevented the Austrians profiting by the hurried retreat of the French centre, and lost them the opportunity of inflicting a severe loss upon the enemy. The archduke's fetters were of his own making: and the Aulic Council have enough to answer for, without fathering the effects of that timid and dilatory system of war, of which Mr. Alison's beau ideal of a chief is at once the greatest example and advocate.

Mr. Alison, continuing to represent the Aulic Council as the scapegoat for all the archduke's shortcomings as a general, proceeds in his sixth volume, under the head of "Operations in Germany" after Stockach, and with the date of the 13th April, to say:—

In vain the archduke urged the Aulic Council not to lose the precious moment: they desired not to endanger the advantages which they had already gained—enjoined him to confine his operations to clearing the right bank of the Danube by detached parties.

Now, we cannot understand here how the Aulic Council could have issued these instructions, seeing that, at the period mentioned, there was not a single Frenchman on the right bank of the Danube; but supposing, as we do, that Mr. Alison has here spoken of the Danube when he must mean the Rhine, we no less demur to accept his conclusion, that the Aulic Council are chargeable as the impediment to the archduke's proceedings at this moment; when we read in the archduke's own words:—

> The archduke had fixed on the 10th April to commence his operations on Zurich, with which Hotze was to combine, by advancing from the Vorarlberg by St. Gall; but at the moment when the troops were about to move, the inspector-general of provisions declared it impossible to furnish the requisite supplies. This obstacle, nevertheless, could not have proved insurmountable in so fertile a land as Suabia, if other circumstances had not stopped the Austrian Army in the course of their success. The illness of the Archduke Charles forced him to give over the command of the army, for some time, to General Wallis; during which, considerable reinforcements of French troops arriving in Alsace, and about Mayence and Manheim, caused doubts as to their destination, &c.

Surely the Aulic Council should not be held responsible for the deficiencies of the archduke's commissary-general, or the state of His Highness's health, which are thus plainly stated by the best possible authority to have cost "the precious moment," for which he has declared the council responsible. Mr. Alison's context after the quotation, given at the beginning of this paragraph, goes on to say:—

> After several engagements, the French were finally expelled from the German side . . . Masséna found himself, by these disasters, under the necessity of changing entirely the disposition of his army. Turned, on the one flank by the Imperialists, on the lake of Constance, and on the other by the advance of Kray beyond the Adige, he was compelled to retire into the central part of Switzerland."

Now, of the engagements and disasters to which Mr. Alison refers, we have the following account from the Archduke Charles:—

> The Austrians allowed the whole month of April to glide away in blameable inaction. Their advance guards alone amused

themselves by driving the enemy on the 13th from Schaffhaus-
en—the 14th from Petershausen—the 17th from Eglisau, and
clearing the right bank of the Rhine.

These dates are days of April, on the 6th of which month Kray had
finally passed the Adige; but so far from Masséna being compelled to
retire into the central part of Switzerland by these operations, we find
Mr. Alison, in the next page, describing the position of his army with
its right in the Tyrol and the rest along the Rhine, from the Grisons to
Bâsle; and further, that its posts were not withdrawn from the left bank
of that river till the 20th May, and then not on account of the operations
alluded to by Mr. Alison, but in consequence of its right being turned
by Hotze and Bellegarde falling on it from the Tyrol, and the archduke
crossing the river in co-operation with them: but this was late in May,
and circumstances were vastly changed in these five weeks. Masséna
bore himself nobly under his difficulties when they beset him; but he
would have been a fool, or worse, to have fallen back to the centre of
Switzerland, at the period and for the reasons adduced by Mr. Alison.

After having thus stated that Masséna was compelled to retire into
the centre of Switzerland by the archduke's successes in Germany and
Kray's passing the Adige, Mr. Alison, in his sixth volume, contradicts
himself, by admitting that it was through the successes of Bellegarde
and Hotze that the right wing of Masséna was forced to retire from
the Tyrol and the Grisons; adding, as a consequence of these movements, that:—

The Imperialists were interposed in a salient angle between the
Republican armies, the one thrown back on the line of the Po,
the other on that of the Aar. Moreau succeeded Scherer in the
command of the army of Italy at this momentous crisis . . . . . .
and after a vain attempt to maintain the line of the Oglio, the
troops retired towards Milan. . . . Moreau finding himself, &c.
&c., resolved to retire towards the mountains of Genoa, in order
to facilitate his junction with Macdonald.

And, at greater length than we can afford, Mr. Alison goes on to
show Moreau making his arrangements for the defence of the Adda.
The wording of this passage would represent Moreau's assumption of
the command in Italy as subsequent to, or simultaneous with, Bellegarde's successes in the Grisons, whereas it was three weeks anterior to
them; and by the time they were effected, Moreau, so far from making
an attempt to hold the line of the Oglio, was in the Maritime Alps,

near Mondovi and Coni.

But the important error here maintained is, that Moreau commanded the French on the Oglio, and planned the reprehensible dispositions for defending the Adda; whereas Mr, Alison's authority, the Archduke Charles, would have told him that General Scherer did all this—giving over the command to Moreau on the 25th April, the day on which Suwarow's army reached the Adda to attack Lecco on the morrow. Monsieur Thiers goes still further, saying that Scherer:—

> Having altogether lost his wits, occupied the line of the Adda in the most unfortunate manner; and that on the 27th April, in the evening, at the very moment that the line was forced, he handed over the command of the army to Moreau.

Scherer's dispositions for defending the Adda, followed immediately as they were by Moreau's for the defence of the Po and Tanaro, one would have thought sufficient to manifest to Mr. Alison, and to have called for inculcation on his readers, that difference in the two men which was already evident to Kray before these operations, when he said:—

> *Si leur général est Scherer, je le battrai; si c'est Moreau, nous nous battrons.*

Later Mr. Alison, as already mentioned, states that Suwarow "for above a week gave himself up to festivities at Milan," and again, in his seventh volume, he repeats that "Suwarow, by an undue delay of eight days at Milan, missed the opportunity of destroying the French Army"—whereas, entering Milan, as he did, on the 29th April, we find his letters and despatches dated from Lodi on the 1st May; and we also read, in the archduke's work, that "the allies, 44,000 strong, left Milan on the 1st May, and Suwarow moved on Pavia."

Mr. Alison, on the contrary, describes him, after this imaginary week's festivities, "at length, wearied with triumphal honours, setting out for Alexandria;" to which he did not go at all during this period of the campaign. In the following page, Mr. Alison, having brought Suwarow to Tortona, says, that:

> To divert his enemy's attention, he extended his right from Novi to Seravalle and Gavi, threatening thereby his communications with Genoa and France; but that this was a mere feint, intended to mask his real design, which was to cross the Po, turn his left, and force him to a general and decisive action.

To which we would respectfully observe, that if his object was to divert the enemy by extending his right from Novi to Serravalle, he would very probably have succeeded; as, to have done so, he must have forced his army to the right about, or countermarched it, presenting its back to the astonished enemy. But supposing, as we do here, a mistake of right for left, and that the movement in question would have threatened Moreau's communication with Genoa, what, in the name of strategy! could it have to do with his communications with France, which were carried on by the Mont Cenis and the Col de Tende?

Nor can we subscribe to Mr. Alison's concluding observation in this passage, as it is most distinctly made manifest by Suwarow's orders and letters, that, from the time he turned towards Moreau at San Salvadore, his object was to attack or turn his right; for which purpose he ordered Rosenberg to pass over from the left bank of the Po and join him; and that when he found this too difficult, or inexpedient, he gave up the idea of attacking him at all, and crossed the Po with his main body; not to force him to a battle, but to march on Turin, and to leave Moreau, for the time, to his own devices; no part of his main army moving towards Moreau till the 2nd June, a fortnight after he crossed the Po to move on Turin.

In the following page, we find Mr. Alison writing, that, after the affair of Basignano or Mugarone, on the 12th May:—

> The Allied Army was concentrated anew in the entrenched camp of Garofalo. At the same instant that this was passing in one quarter, Suwarow raised his camp at San Juliano, with the design of crossing the Po, near Casa Tenia, and marching upon Sesia. The attempt was not attended with decisive success: a warm action ensued between the division of Victor and the Russian advanced guard, 9,000 strong, under Generals Bagration and Lusignan; victory was long doubtful, and although the French were at length forced to retreat, under shelter of the cannon of Alexandria, the demonstration led to no serious impression at the time on the position of the Republican general. Tired with the unsatisfactory nature of these manoeuvres, Suwarow resolved to march with the bulk of his forces on Turin.

This is really the most curious piece of history, of its length, that ever was written. It represents, if I understand it aright, that the troops at Garofalo and San Juliano were two distinct bodies, the former of which remained in its entrenched camp, while the latter broke up to march upon a place called Sesia: with some intention, that, though not decisively successful, led to an action, the result of which, though the French were driven back, produced no impression at the time on Moreau's position; and that Suwarow, apparently baffled, then resolved to march on Turin. Whereas the real facts are, that the troops at Garofalo and San Juliano (the latter being an outpost of the former) were alike connected portions of Suwarow's main army, which broke up on the 16th May (not with the remotest idea of disturbing Moreau—in fact, to march away from before him), under distinct and published orders to march on Turin, passing the intermediate River Sesia *en route*; and that as their rear-guard (not their advanced-guard—which was already crossing the Po), under Lusignan and Bagration, was preparing at San Juliano to obey this order, it was attacked by Moreau, who advanced from San Salvadore, crossing the Tanaro and Bormida Rivers, to make a strong reconnoissance in this direction.

The repulse of Moreau, so far from leading to no serious impression on his position at the time, led him to break up his camp the very next day, sending Victor with his infantry to Genoa, and abandoning it himself on the following morning with the rest of his army, by forced marches, on Asti and Moncaglieri; while Suwarow deliberately proceeded with his march on the Sesia and Turin (an identical operation—not two distinct ones, as described by Mr. Alison), which was in progress before, and in a degree interrupted (*i.e.*, by the detention of the troops while beating the enemy) by the demonstration made by Moreau (not by Suwarow), and not in the remotest degree originated, as Mr. Alison states, in Suwarow's dissatisfaction at the victory which had punished his enemy's accidental interference with its proceedings. Mr. Alison says:—

It was agreed that Macdonald should cross the Apennines and advance towards Tortona, his right resting on the mountains— his left, on the right bank of the Po.

Here Mr. Alison by right means left, and by left means right, or we very much mistake his tactical notions; and at the succeeding page, when he writes, that "Suwarow ordered up great part of the garrison of Mantua to reinforce his army," it would puzzle anyone, aware that the said garrison were all French, and enemies to Suwarow, if the frequency of lapses of this kind in Mr. Alison's history had not pretty well broken in the reader to the habit of interpreting Mr. Alison's small errors of haste, by believing them to involve a meaning as opposite as possible to that they stand for.

Again, a few lines only before the last quotation alluded to, Mr. Alison, to establish a comparison between Napoleon operating against Wurmser and Suwarow, at the Trebbia, makes the very extraordinary assertion, that:—

> The Russian general, though at the head of an army considerably inferior to that of his adversaries, was superior everywhere at the decisive point. The citadel of Turin, with its immense magazines, was captured by an army of only 40,000 men, in presence of two whose united force exceeded 50,000.

Now, putting Kray's forces out of the calculation, and with every inclination to say all that can fairly be urged in glorification of Suwarow, we have only to open Mr. Alison's own account of the respective numbers of these armies, to show the emptiness of this gratuitous affirmation. Allowing Moreau and Macdonald to have had 50,000 men, we find opposed to them, and besieging Turin the following array:—Suwarow at Garofalo 36,000; 6,000 under Ott, who joined Suwarow at the Tidone; five battalions and six squadrons, say 4,000 men, who joined in the Trebbia, making a force of 46,000 under Suwarow, while Bellegarde's force opposed to Moreau, Mr. Alison calls four brigades, and the archduke numbers at 8,000 men, besides Wuckassovich's brigade; to which must be added the troops under Kaim besieging the citadel of Turin, which neither Mr. Alison nor the archduke give in numbers, but which the journal of the siege given by the chief engineer, Harting, states to have been 7,415 men.

Here are more than 60,000 shown to have composed Suwarow's operating force, instead of 40,000, as above stated; and what makes this hasty, dashing disregard of calculation provoking in this history is, that, shaking one's confidence in Mr. Alison's statement as it does, it obliges one to stop to investigate the details of any and all of his assertions that are not self-demonstrative.

In his seventh volume (from which volume our subsequent quotations from his work will henceforth be taken), he states that after the surrender of Alexandria, Suwarow, under the date of the 2nd August, "drew his forces round Coni, and commenced the siege of Tortona." Here we are led to conjecture that in his haste Mr. Alison has written Coni for Novi—and if we are wrong in this supposition, we know not what he can mean, Coni being far away in the Col de Tende, quite out of any connection with Tortona: besides that in the same page he himself contradicts the statements here objected to, writing, that:—

> The Allies could only muster 45,000 men in front of Tortona:
> General Kaim being at Cherasco with 12,000 to observe the
> army of the Alps; Klenau in Tuscany with 7,000 combatants;
> and the remainder of their great army occupied in keeping up
> the communications between their widely scattered forces.

After giving Suwarow's simple battle-order at Novi,—"Kray and
Bellegarde will attack the left, the Russians the centre, and Melas the
right,"—he acquaints us, that "Suwarow's design was to force back the
right of the French by means of the corps of Kray, while Bagration
had orders to turn their left;" proceeding to illustrate this direct contradiction of Suwarow's design, by describing Kray's attack upon the
left of the French Army.

In speaking of the crowning and crushing error of the campaign
of 1799,—*viz.*, the departure of the Archduke Charles, with the great
body of the Austrian Army from Switzerland, before Suwarow's arrival in that country,—Mr. Alison pronounces that at the critical moment of Hotze's defeat at Näefels (30th August):—

> The archduke, yielding to the pressing commands of the Aulic
> Council, was compelled to abandon the army with the great
> body of his troops, leaving the united force of Korsakow and
> Hotze, 56,000 strong, scattered over a line forty miles in length,
> to sustain the weight of Masséna, who could bring 65,000 to
> bear upon the decisive point around the ramparts of Zurich.

From this assertion we need scarcely say we entirely dissent. In
the foregoing sketch, we have already given Lord Mulgrave's declaration, and Cobentzel's detailed explanation to the Emperor Paul, of
the views of the Austrian Cabinet, that the archduke should remain
in Switzerland till Suwarow should arrive there; and as further proof,
we add the following extract from the Emperor Francis's letter to
Suwarow, dated the 27th August:—

> I have charged my brother, the Archduke Charles, to throw
> back the enemy, and replace the former state of things (*i.e.*, to
> recover the line of the St. Gothard, lost by the left of his army
> on the 16th August), since these unfortunate events would en-
> tail the worst consequences, and might cost the loss of all our
> advantages in Switzerland.

Surely this declaration, written from Vienna on the 27th August, is utterly incompatible with the transmission of any previous orders sent from thence, which could compel the Archduke Charles to quit that country with his army, as he did on the 29th, 30th, and 31st of the same month.

We apprehend that Mr. Alison has misled himself in this matter by the apparent authority of the quotation which he gives from the archduke's work, to the effect that "the Court of Vienna ordered the immediate execution of its will, without further objections;" but if Mr. Alison will carefully examine the archduke's history, he will see that in discussing the general plan agreed upon, the archduke dissented from it *in toto*, considered his ultimate destination to the Lower Rhine as faulty, showing how preferable it would be for his whole army, united to all the Russians, to act in Switzerland; and after commenting on the folly of statesmen far from the scene of war deciding on military operations, records the failure of his reasoning in the words, "*la Cour de Vienne ordonne le secret, et la prompte exécution de ses voluntés sans aucune objection,*" *i.e.* the Cabinet adhered to the general plan, the most prominent and important feature of which we have seen to be the maintenance of things *in statu quo* in Switzerland by the archduke, till Suwarow should arrive there.

The decision of the Vienna Cabinet had reached the archduke before Masséna's attack upon his left or the arrival of Korsakow (*Campagne de 1799*); but so far from compelling him to quit Switzerland post haste, we find him, as soon as Korsakow had arrived, engaged, with his whole army, in his abortive attempt to pass the Aar on the 16th August: the success of which would have led him on Berne and Geneva; and after that failure on the 21st commencing an operation on his left, to recover the ground it had lost on the 16th.

But the force he sent under Hotze was insufficient for its purpose, and when Korsakow, with his whole army had moved on the 25th to co-operate with Hotze, the archduke and he squabbled about the removal of six Austrian battalions, which the archduke withdrew from the scene of action; the result of this wretched puerility was, that the archduke, disgusted and unable to command either himself or Korsakow, incontinently took himself off abruptly to the theatre of war, for which he had been told he was ultimately destined. His own description of his motives runs thus:—

Time was being uselessly lost—the enemy was receiving reinforcements every day, and Germany was more and more threatened. It was idle to expect the re-establishment of that harmony which, even under most favourable auspices, seldom lasts long between allied armies, and which alone could form one powerful mass of the forces scattered in Germany and Switzerland. Under these considerations, the archduke thought it best to follow the orders of his court, and to abandon to chance what henceforth would not depend on him.

We look upon the archduke's proceeding at this moment as one of the most flagrant and reckless ebullitions of a little mind that history anywhere exhibits. He had a general instruction to move to Germany, when the security of Switzerland would allow him so to do; and showing clearly by his operations from the 16th to the 25th of August that he knew it was his duty not to quit it till he had at least done what he was ordered to do, he abruptly left it at the end of August; though, on the 30th of that month, Masséna made a general movement against the whole line of the combined Austrian and Russian Armies, signally defeating a portion of the former.

Seeing thus unquestionably that Masséna was so strong as to court a conflict with their whole united force, the archduke chose this moment to remove from it thirty battalions and forty-two squadrons, with the object of assembling more than 70,000 men in Germany, where 12,000 French had crossed the Rhine! Mr. Alison says, he was compelled to do this by pressing orders from the Aulic Council, quoting in his margin the 129th, 135th, and 139th pages from the archduke's work, as authorities for the statement; which we here deliberately assert to be in no manner borne out by these or any other pages of the archduke's history.

We take this opportunity to assert, that, however detrimental the general effect of the interference of the Aulic Council at Vienna may have been on the operations of 1799, the only leader of the Allies who (we suppose through the influence of his rank as brother of the emperor) took upon himself to set them at nought, was the Archduke Charles. We find His Highness stating, (first volume):—

It directed him to await the arrival of the Russians, though they could not be on the Rhine till July, before he entered Switzerland from Suabia.

But we know he entered Switzerland on the 22nd May. He himself declares how cavalierly he disregarded their orders when he attempted the great operation of the Aar, he says:—

The probable result of the projected enterprise offered a brilliant prospect. Its success might have obtained his pardon for not having followed to the letter the instructions he had received. Probably, they would not have stopped him or turned him from the object to which he was rapidly advancing.

All we read of authority distinctly states, that the archduke was ordered to remain in Switzerland, or to leave it secure till Suwarow's arrival; and we have seen how he disobeyed that order, while in the case of the relief of Haddick's corps, which he was directed to effect early in the campaign, he doggedly refused compliance from first to last, in direct defiance of orders from the council and the emperor, and of the reiterated, though politely worded, remonstrances of Suwarow. His Highness's version of this act is curiously cool. Acknowledging that these troops were:—

To be replaced by detachments taken from Northern Switzerland. The archduke represented the danger of removing troops from the key of the theatre of war, by detaching them to the south, and the ordered relief did not take place; so that the Russian general was obliged to employ an equal number of troops to those he had called to him to cover his flank, &c.

As a contrast to Mr. Alison's *beau-ideal* of a general, we produce Suwarow's letter to the archduke of the 30th June, on this subject:—

Supposing that the order of his Imperial Majesty for the relief of Haddick's corps by that of Hotze would have been immediately executed, I withdrew Haddick and a part of his troops to my army, ordering the remainder to follow when relieved. As, however, Your Imperial Highness has informed me that the enemy has been reinforced in Switzerland, I have ordered Haddick to resume his position; at the same time observing to Your Highness that I make this arrangement, trusting that, under more favourable circumstances, Your Imperial Highness's orders will be given for an immediate fulfilment of the desire of the illustrious emperor. But nothing of the sort happened, and Suwarow had to grumble at the loss of 15,000 men to the end of the campaign.

Suwarow not being the emperor's brother, but simply a good soldier, dared not imitate this stylish way of illustrating the military duty of obedience, but did great things in spite of all the hampering of the Aulic Council. As the archduke depreciatingly remarks, in speaking of a childish dissemination of the Italian forces, "*Suwarow s'en tint scrupuleusement à ses instructions.*" This I call a real soldier, that no *beau-ideal* of Mr. Alison's standard can ever match. As an additional illustration of this view, we would call attention to the archduke's plea for his conduct, of the difficulty to him of preserving harmony with his Allies; and to his further comment on this peculiar, and to him insurmountable, obstacle to success, which Mr. Alison dignifies with the epithet "profound."

We, on the contrary, deem them shallow in the extreme, and refer for their practical refutation to the uninterrupted harmony and unity of action displayed by the Austrian and Russian forces under Suwarow, from their junction at Valeggio till they separated at Alexandria. The difficulties which crushed the archduke to a nullity in the nine days from the 16th to the 25th August, were for months neutralised by the commanding genius of Suwarow; or rather converted to a means of unvarying and resplendent triumphs. Entrusted with precisely similar materials, the latter produced the fusion which spoke the master in his art; the former the confusion which betrayed the bungler. If a man cannot drive a spirited team, he has no business on the coach-box.

Mr. Alison proceeds to inform us, that:—

> The arrival of the archduke was soon attended with important effects on the Upper Rhine. The French had crossed that river at Manheim with 12,000 men, and driving General Müller, who commanded the Imperialists, before them, laid siege to Philipsburg.

The important effects alluded to, were the retreat of these 12,000 men, on learning that the archduke had honoured them by assembling full 70,000 to deal with them, and the subsequent capture of Manheim; which the archduke acknowledges to have been an afterthought, when he found there was nothing else to do with his enormous force; somewhat naively confessing, that when he left Switzerland, it was with no immediate object but that of remaining idle for some time about the sources of the Danube. But we have alluded to this passage, to remark that what Mr. Alison calls the Upper Rhine, is what, in military parlance, is usually styled the Middle Rhine; and that his description of the French driving General Müller, who commanded the Imperialists, before them, is slightly at variance with the account of the archduke and other military historians: they represent that general as having been the commander of the French, who drove, and not of the Imperialists who were driven, on this occasion. But Müller looks like a German name, and Mr. Alison will write hastily.

Mr. Alison pronounces Masséna to be "the first general then in Europe," which seems somewhat at variance with his classification, at the subsequent page, of Suwarow and the archduke as two of the "four commanders who in the age of the French Revolution have risen to the highest eminence." The other two being Wellington and Napoleon.

In narrating the St. Gothard movement, Mr. Alison describes Suwarow as arriving at Airolo on the 21st, and not attacking it till two days after. This delay, if avoidable, would have been faulty; but Suwarow's letters and reports, as well as the archduke's relation, show that it never occurred; but that, leaving Taverne on the 21st, he marched every day, falling on Airolo the very moment he reached it.

Mr. Alison altogether nullifies Lecourbe's splendid extrication of himself, when enclosed between Suwarow at Hospital and Rosenberg at Andermatt, on the night of the 24th September, by stating that he broke down the Devil's Bridge, and this, too, subsequently to his throwing his artillery into the Reuss and retiring down the valley of Schollenen; whereas it was the blowing up of the Devil's Bridge by the fugitives driven back by Rosenberg, which compromised Lecourbe, by destroying the only apparent means of retreat for him, from the Urseren Valley; and it was his glorious decision on hearing this confounding event, which forms one of the most brilliant traits of his unequalled fame as an Alpine general. If Lecourbe had had the breaking down of the bridge, it would have been surprising he did not take his artillery over it before he destroyed it.

We find in the next page Mr. Alison speaking of the route of the Allies:—

"Lying through the horrible defile of the Schachenthal, in which even the audacious Lecourbe had not ventured to engage his troops, however long habituated to mountain warfare." Respecting which epithet of "horrible" I may observe, that a lady, who had ridden beside me through the whole length of the Schachenthal without once dismounting, having asked me what Mr. Alison could mean by calling it "horrible," I could only answer that "I really did not know." As a soldier, I must venture to observe that Lecourbe did engage his troops in it—as why he should not, I cannot, for the soul of me, imagine,—so soon as it was his duty to do so; but that, at the time of which Mr. Alison speaks, he showed his skill as a general by preferring to hold the post of Seedorf: which Mr. Alison might have learned from his great authority, the archduke, "gave him a threatening air, and was a post from which he could disturb all Suwarow's movements.

In describing the Russian march out of the Schachenthal and over the Kinziculm, Mr. Alison says:—

No words can do justice to the difficulties experienced in this terrible march, or the heroism of the brave men engaged in it.

This, with the rest of his description, I hold to be extravagant exaggeration: the march was, as I have endeavoured to describe it a stiff mountain walk of six or seven hours, undertaken at the best season of the year, and without an enemy on the line. Here and there it is difficult, for a horse unaccustomed to mountain paths, but to talk of it as terrible, or of the heroism of the men who took this walk, is simple twaddle. The pastures above Mutten, to within a short hour's walk of the village, belong to the Uri or Schachenthal people; and every man, woman, child, goat, or cow, that has to do with them, pass and repass the whole distance incessantly, during the summer.

The morning I walked it, I passed at least a dozen men and women heavily laden with cheese, &c., going or returning over the culm; and certainly neither they nor I seemed to fancy that our heroism was at all taxed, in dealing either with the ups or downs of the pastures, or of the rugged bits that intervene between them. As a difficult or trying march, it is mere child's play to the marches of Lecourbe's people over the glaciers of the Grimsel, or those above Martinsbrück, or twenty others made in these campaigns by detachments of either army.

The last objection I have to urge to Mr. Alison's views on the operations we have canvassed, is that, he extenuates the conduct of the Austrian General Linken, by describing the situation of the French General Molitor as all but desperate; and adding "by a little more vigour on the part of the Russians, it might have been rendered so." Putting out of consideration the fact that it was no part of the combined plan that the Russians should have appeared at all in the quarter in question, Mr. Alison himself stating that Linken was to have joined them at Mutten, we would ask how, by any additional vigour, the Russians—arriving after this terrible march, as Mr. Alison calls it, at Mutten on the 28th, and moving next day to the Klonthal (a stiffish march) where they were momentarily checked—could have rendered Molitor's situation more desperate; when Linken had allowed himself to be driven, or rather had fallen back without being pursued, to the baths of Wichlen, at the further end of the Sernfthal?

Mr. Alison is quite singular in this strange view; as even the Archduke Charles clearly points out where the fault really lay: in the first instance, in the attacks of Jellachich and Linken not being simultaneous; and, secondly, in the latter general quitting the scene of action unnecessarily.

An officer entrusted with a co-operative movement should never, unless forced to do so by superior numbers, either pass from the offensive to the defensive, or withdraw from the operation of which he is a part; so long as there is a doubt on his mind with regard to the abandonment of the enterprise.

The simple fact that Molitor turned from pursuing him, was proof positive that either the Russians or Jellachich were finding him work to do. The want of vigour in these operations was an Austrian, not a Russian deficiency.

In the foregoing notices, I have endeavoured to justify my apparent presumption in rejecting the authority of so celebrated a writer as Mr. Alison; whom I cannot but consider careless and hasty, alike in the formation of his opinions and his statements of facts; and I the more lament the very extensive exhibition of these deficiencies in his work (numerous instances of which have been flagrantly exposed in the pages of the *United Service Magazine*), because I honour him for the ability, and the healthy tone of sentiment and feeling often apparent in its pages.

I need not repeat here that I dissent, *in extenso,* from Mr. Alison's extreme eulogies on the perfect character and consummate Generalship of the Archduke Charles. That he was a good man, I believe: though I think the authority adduced by Mr. Alison to establish the fact—*viz.*, that of Napoleon—the very worst in Europe that could be brought in favour of it; because when, as Mr. Alison informs us:—

Jealousy towards everyone who had either essentially injured or rivalled his reputation, and a total disregard of truth when recounting their operations, are two of his defects.

I am inclined to think his good word is as likely to be biased as his bad one; and I read in other historians that the archduke lowered

193

himself, and injured his country, by the slavish admiration with which he regarded and flattered Napoleon. I also believe he had great gifts as a leader: but I do not think with Mr. Alison, that his campaign of 1796, was equal to Napoleon's; that his retreat in 1797, was so able as to procure for his country a more advantageous peace than she would have had without it; that, but for the Aulic Council, he would have achieved the subversion of the French Republic in 1799; or that, but for the neglect of the Archduke John, he would have crushed Napoleon at Wagram, as decisively as Wellington and Blücher did at Waterloo. These are Mr. Alison's declarations, from which I dissent. What follows, are opinions on the Archduke Charles, in which I concur.

In 1796:—

Le jeune Archiduc dût au vue du plan François, une belle pensée qu'il exécuta avec prudence: mais, comme Moreau, il manqua de cette ardeur, de cette audace, qui pouvoit rendre la faute du gouvernement François mortelle pour ses armées. Conçoit on ce qui serait arrivé si d'un côté ou de l'autre, s'était trouvé le génie impétueux qui venait de détruire trois armées au delà des Alpes! Cette campagne valut en Europe une grande réputation au jeune Archiduc.—Thiers,

In 1797, the archduke was driven, by an uninterrupted succession of defeats, from the Tagliamento to beyond Klagenfürth in the short space of three weeks; and I look in vain to the pages of every historian within my reach, for any proof of the particular ability assumed for this operation by Mr. Alison, Colonel Mitchell says of the archduke at this period:—

The youth, rank, bravery, and success of this prince disposed the troops to place the greatest confidence in him; and had he combined popular qualities, and a just insight into character, with the talents and acquirements he certainly possessed, he might very possibly have acted a splendid part in the history of his time. But along with abilities, there was evidently some want of decision or power of acting, as well as an absence of the manners which gain the soldier's heart.

Mr. Alison's slashing declaration, that, but for the Aulic Council, the archduke would have subverted France in 1799, is a bold inference from a series of operations perhaps the lamest, most bungling, and least marked with the display of military qualities, that were ever perpetrated by a constantly superior force under a general of note; concluding precisely on the ground on which they commenced, *viz.*, between the Danube and the Lake of Constance. I cannot better convey my idea of its value than by paraphrasing Gibbon's query:—

But who will answer for Abu Taleb?

The archduke, in 1809, after his defeats at Abonsberg and Ech-mühl, had a glorious chance afforded him by the breaking of Napoleon's bridges on the Danube, leaving only a portion of his army at Aspern and Essling; but he had not energy to seize the advantages thus literally placed before him. Read Masséna's opinion:—

Je ne conçois rien à la conduite de l'Archiduc Charles: on disait que ce prince avait des talents militaires; mais à défaut de talents, il suffisait de l'experience qu'il a dû acquérir en faisant la guerre, pour lui faire un grand succés dans la bataille d'hier.

The same opinion is thus expressed by the historian Capefigue:—

Si l'Archiduc Charles n'avait pas eu cette timidité de toute sa vie militaire, il eut acculé l'armée sur le Danube. Il recula encore une fois devant sa destinée, le nom de l'Empereur lui inspirait trop d'enthousiasme militaire—il avait le respect de l'éleve pour le mâitre. Le prince manqua donc de vigueur!

The same want of vigour which cramped the archduke's success at Aspern, was Napoleon's encouragement to the daring measure of occupying Lobau till his reinforcements should join him, he says:—

L'Archiduc Charles est toujours hésitant devant moi: les Autrichiens ont un grand respect pour la capacité et la supériorité des troupes Françaises. Si ce prestige s'evanouit, que restera-t-il?

This conjecture was so borne out by the subsequent inactivity of the archduke, that "*l'immobilité inexplicable de l'Archiduc*," and "torpor or stupefaction appears to have fallen upon him," are the similar expressions of historians, the most opposite in their national and natural biases. Leaving Mr. Alison's *dictum* as to the result of Wagram in the event of what did not happen, we quote from Capefigue its real sequel:—

Le Prince Charles reprochait à l'Archiduc Jean de n'être arrive que tardiraent sur le champ de bataille, et il avait raison: Jean à son tour reprochait à son ainé de n'avoir pas profité d'Essling, et de la première journée de Wagram. La modestie extrême du Prince Charles lui faisoit croire que nul ne pouvoit disputer la victoire à Napoléon: il n'avait pas

foi en soi-même, et son inquiétude des suites de cette guerre devint telle,
qu'il donna sa démission en pleine compagne, découragement qui n'a
pas d'exemple!

Unless we see something very much of the same character in his
abrupt departure from Switzerland because the game did not play as
he would have it.

Briefly, to me the character of the archduke, as displayed by Capefigue, looks far more like truth than that so positively and saliently
dashed off by Mr. Alison:—

L'Archiduc avait fait de sérieuses études; il appartenait encore à la
vieille stratégie, prudente et timide; pour ne rien hazarder il perdait
souvent les chances de la fortune et de la victoire. Sa loyauté extrême
admirait, avec une candeur digne d'éloges, les qualités militaires de
l'Empereur Français: cette admiration poussée à un degré trop exalté ne
convenait pas dans une guerre ou il fallait plus combattre l'ennemi, que
s'enthousiasmer pour son chef. L'Archiduc Charles comme toutes les
supériorités avait des exigences, des systèmes, et il voulait être le maitre
des opérations d'une campagne. Il n'avoit rien de cette force morale qui
sauve les empires; il ne savait prendre aucune de ses résolutions qui
donnent à une cause une grande énergie: brave de sa personne, tacticien
distingué, il savait conduire une armèe, la faire vaincre quelquefois; mais
son esprit étoit pusillanime et incapable d'une résolution bardie; de là,
toutes ces dissensions nées parmi généraux Autrichiens et les Archiducs
même. Ce fut un singulier caractère que celui de l'Archiduc Charles:
bon patriote Autrichien, avec cela timide, faisant la guerre pour obtenir
la paix: disposé à, tout céder: admiration du génie de Napoléon, se
posant devant lui avec une modestie si résignée qu'il compromettait
souvent la destinée d'une campagne par de fausses démarchbes. Les
deux hommes les plus nuisibles à la grandeur militaire de l'Autriche
furent l'Archiduc Charles et le Prince Jean de Licbstentein, tous deux
avec de beaux talents mais sans caractère politique."

I need not say that, adopting as I do this opinion of the Archduke
Charles, I cannot acquiesce in Mr. Alison's view, that the archduke
"was the general of all others, in those days of glory, who approached
nearest to the standard of ideal perfection," nor look on him for a
moment as a leader to be considered under the same category as Napoleon or Wellington.

Bismark says:—

The qualifications which a consummate general should possess, may be divided into two branches, one of which can be acquired, but the other must be innate: that is, into the scientific part, or that which can be mathematically constructed; and into the philosophical part, or that which depends upon the sound judgment of a well-regulated understanding. The difference is as great as that between knowledge of a thing, and ability to carry it into execution; but the possession of one only of these qualities falls short of the *ideal*, and both *united in common* are indispensable to form the perfect general.

The sympathies of my feelings and judgment alike incline me to be partial to Suwarow; and yet I see in him a general of a secondary class, because decision and energy, and the power of exciting the average qualities of a mass of men to absolute devotion, will not, without correct strategical ideas and due considerate foresight, establish him as a perfect leader. Still less do I think that all the archduke's knowledge of strategy, and far-looking consideration—shackled, as it was, by the want of decision and energy, which so often made him listless with world-winning opportunities before him, and by the poverty of mind which could neither conciliate nor command the powers entrusted to his guidance—can entitle him to the rank of a first-rate leader.

Suwarow, with all his failings, was never defeated; and once only baffled, through the acknowledged failure of others' co-operation. The archduke's first campaign was his only successful one, and military critics largely ascribe the causes of the ill success of more than one of his others to his want of true military qualities.

His most palpable deficiency was the want of that "barbarian energy" he disliked in the Russians. Whether he really undervalued it, or felt like Saxe, (though he would not admit, like him) that the quality conspicuous in others was unattainable by himself or his people, I know not; but the result is certain: that, whereas the Russians bore up nobly through good and ill fortune, so as eventually to fight their way to Paris; the archduke's opinions, personal and professional, banished him from the theatre of war when war became most glorious, and gave him only the fame of a "great arithmetician," while Europe was lost and won almost within his hearing of the *mêlée*. He indulged a too susceptible sensitiveness, at the cost of a chance of becoming one of the foremost names of history.

A few days since, on looking at a very clever novel by Mr. G. H.

Lewes, I found, in better words than I am master of, a perfect exposition of the abstract ideas on which I ground my decided preference of Suwarow over the archduke. This gentleman writes:—

Strength of will, is the quality most needing cultivation in mankind. Will is the central force which gives strength and greatness to character. We overestimate the value of talent, because it dazzles us; and we are apt to underrate the importance of will, because its works are less shining. Talent gracefully adorns life, but it is will which carries us victoriously through the struggle. Intellect is the torch which lights us on our way; will, the strong arm which rough-hews the path for us. The clever weak man sees all the obstacles on his path: the very torch he carries, being brighter than that of most men, enables him perhaps to see that the path before him may be directest, the best, yet it also enables him to see the crooked turnings by which he may, as he fancies, reach the goal without encountering difficulties. If, indeed, intellect were a sun instead of a torch—if it irradiated every corner and crevice—then would man see how, in spite of every obstacle, the direct path was the only safe one, and he would cut his way through by manful labour. But, constituted as we are, it is the clever, weak men who stumble most—the strong men who are most virtuous and happy. In this world there cannot be virtue without strong will. The weak 'know the right, and yet the wrong pursue.'

www.ingramcontent.com/pod-product-compliance
Lightning Source LLC
Chambersburg PA
CBHW021056090426
42738CB00006B/371